A Methodist Guide
to Cornwall

Compiled by Thomas Shaw

Second revised edition edited by Colin Short

Methodist
Publishing House

First edition copyright © Thomas Shaw 1991
This edition updated 2005 copyright © Joan Shaw/Colin Short
Cover photography © Joan Shaw

British Library Cataloguing in Publication data

A catalogue record for this book is available from the British Library

ISBN 1 85852 263 3

First published by
Methodist Publishing House
4 John Wesley Road
Werrington
Peterborough PE4 6ZP

Foreword

For over a decade, Thomas Shaw's excellent book has been an invaluable guide for all who have wanted to explore the riches of Cornwall's Methodist heritage. Many people are aware of Gwennap Pit and the Wesley Cottage at Trewint, but this guide has enabled countless individuals and groups to discover so much more of the Methodist tradition which has played such an important part in the development of Cornwall since the time of John Wesley himself.

This edition, revised and updated by Colin Short, will enable visitors and local people to continue to discover more of Cornwall's Methodist past and the continuing influence of that heritage in the county today. As the various Methodist sites are explored, there will be the opportunity to encounter, interwoven inevitably with the history, the powerful message of the Good News of Jesus – a message which changed lives in the past and a message which is changing lives still today.

This new edition is to be published in 2005 – a year in which the Methodist Conference is taking place in the South West. This publication brings together, therefore, an opportunity to understand more clearly the richness of Methodist history with a reminder that, in the debates and decisions of the Conference, the Methodist Church continues today to build on that heritage, seeking still, to 'serve the present age'.

I commend this book to you and pray that as you explore Cornwall's Methodist heritage you may find your faith renewed.

Rev Dr Christopher Blake
Chair of Cornwall District

Contents

Introduction

From 1743, when first Charles and then John Wesley first rode into Cornwall, until the present day, Methodism has made a deep impression on the map of Cornwall, not least by the ubiquitous chapels, both open and closed, which dot the landscape.

A glance at an OS map of Cornwall will show that both full-day and half-day tours can easily be arranged either from a touring centre or from the A30, the major road between Launceston, (pronounced Lanson) and Penzance. The following paragraphs contain suggested tours of particular kinds, and many others can be arranged from the material given in the Gazetteer.

ORDNANCE SURVEY REFERENCES
Most places in the Gazetteer can easily be found on the OS Maps. Grid references are given in some instances to help locate places which, for one reason or another, may prove less easy to find.

THE WESLEY TRAIL
reaches into almost every part of the county. The two main Wesley sites, Trewint and Gwennap Pit, are close to the A30, but there are many other places associated with Wesley, lying along both the north and the south coast routes down to those parts west of Truro where he first established the Methodist societies among the tinners, around Gwennap, Redruth, Pool, Camborne, Hayle, St Ives and St Just. The old mine stacks are still much in evidence in those areas, and places like St Day and St Just still retain the atmosphere of the days of mining prosperity. It was tin and copper mining that made possible the building of the large chapels in those districts, chapels that in some cases were left high and dry when the great mining exodus took place in the last century and transported Cornish Methodism to such places as Grass Valley in California and 'Australia's Little Cornwall'. It is not surprising that Wesley's favourite open-air site in Cornwall (and perhaps in the whole country) is to be found at Gwennap Pit to which the descendants of emigrant Cornish miners from all over the world return year by year.

The eighteenth-century road system through the county can be studied on the copy of Martyn's Map of 1748 in the Methodist Museum at Carharrack. Sections of the roads which Wesley used are still in use, such as the coastal road from St Ives to St Just, the old road from Tresillian to Truro through the Kiggon, and the lane which winds round the Isbell cottage at Trewint. There are numerous parish churches on the Wesley trail which externally have hardly changed in appearance over the centuries, though one has to walk round the north side of Phillack church to recognize it as 'the church in the sandhills' described by an early Primitive Methodist preacher.

The 'Wesley churches' in the north-east of the county, St Gennys, Laneast, Tresmeer, Week St Mary and North Tamerton, are the ones in which he preached; those in the west, such as Zennor, St Buryan, Sancreed and St Just, are the ones where he joined the congregation, often preaching outside after the service. At Endellion, Sancreed, St Agnes, Redruth, Wendron, Launceston, St Austell and St Ives he listened to the local clergy with varying degrees of appreciation which matched their appreciation of his ministry! Few of them chose to sit at his feet as the curate of Truro is depicted doing in the cathedral window!

Houses which Wesley visited can still be seen at Trewint, Mullion, St Just, Rosemergy, Medrose, Cubert, Kenwyn, Altarnun, Mevagissey, Polperro and St Stephen's Coombe. He preached in the town hall at Liskeard and in the still surviving Guildhall at Bodmin. Around St Ives and between Redruth and Helston are a number of rocks, large and small, which are thought to mark Wesley preaching sites. The pulpit at Wesley Rock chapel at Heamoor, Penzance, stands on one of them.

The development of Methodism from a society to a Church is well illustrated at St Just where Wesley's open-air preaching places, his host's house, the society meeting room (c.1746), the first preaching house (1755) and the present Methodist church (1833) can all still be seen. The old chapel at Cubert (c.1765) was bequeathed to the Methodists by Wesley's host.

THE BIBLE CHRISTIANS
One third of Cornish Methodism today is of Bible Christian origin and all over Cornwall there have been chapels bearing date-stones such as the one at Ruthvoes, 'B.C. 1901'. The founder, William O'Bryan, was born at Gunwen, Luxulyan, in 1778 (see William O'Bryan Country p.70).

The well-known and ever popular Billy Bray, who danced along the lanes while one foot shouted 'glo-ary' and the other cried 'hallelujah', was a Bible Christian (see Billy Bray Country p.68).

PRIMITIVE METHODISM
The 'Primitives' in Cornwall had to take 'second place' to the Bible Christians but they became established in the mining areas and in the clay country (see Carn Brea, Phillack and St Ives).

FREE METHODISM
The Wesleyan Methodist Association was introduced to Cornwall (with explosive results in the Camelford Circuit) by the merchant Thomas Pope Rosevear in 1834. From

Camelford it spread to Liskeard and Helston (see Boscastle, Camelford, Treligga, Delabole, Port Isaac, Polperro, Lansallos and Mullion). Samuel Dunn, one of the 'three expelled' Wesleyan ministers of 1849 who became the founders of the United Methodist Free Churches, was born at Mevagissey and, before his expulsion, was Superintendent Minister at Camborne (see Mevagissey, Camborne and Truro Cathedral. For the Teetotal Wesleyan Methodists see St Ives, New Mill and Camborne.) Edward Boaden, born at Cury in 1827, who became the first President of the United Methodist Conference in 1907, was one of the main architects of that union (see Cury).

METHODIST NEW CONNEXION
The New Connexion was rare in Cornwall. Their chapels in the far west largely arose from the Teetotal Wesleyans, and around Truro from disagreements among the Wesleyans in the city (see St Ives, Penzance, Camborne and Truro).

CHAPELS
The chapels can be found everywhere, and the closed ones, now serving other purposes but still bearing marks of their original use, are numerous. Some (ranging from Uncle Frank Tamblyn's chapel at Drift near Liskeard which he built and 'tied to the ground with a bramble' to the vast Italianate UMFC Conference Chapel at Redruth) have been demolished but their sites are often pointed out. Among those still standing in the countryside are many examples of the simple cob and stone-walled buildings such as Gwithian (with its thatched roof) and Porthtowan.

In the towns and old mining centres, such as Camborne, Redruth, Carharrack, Helston and Truro, are imposing buildings which still show some evidence of their original interiors when a slender central pulpit stood in front of a Communion area in an apse. Later Gothic style churches can be seen at Launceston (devoid of its spire), and Penzance (Richmond). Post-war churches are to be found at Saltash, Hayle, Threemilestone and Goldsithney. Stained glass of quality and/or interest is evident at Penzance, (Chapel Street), Helston, Mullion, Mousehole, Newquay and Falmouth. Mousehole and St Blazey Gate (Leek Seed) have pleasing interiors, as also has the little chapel at St Columb.

SURPRISES!
Some of these places have their surprises for the visitor: the pulpit on the rock at Heamoor, the 'Six Johns' commemorated at Mousehole, the Australian tablet at St Erth, the belfry at Port Isaac, the wayside boulders where Wesley preached, the preaching pits, imitating Gwennap, at Indian Queens, Newlyn East and Whitemoor, the five spots of Methodist interest in Truro Cathedral, and the sheer isolation of Innis chapel in the old Quaker burial ground.

HISTORY ALL ROUND

The pilgrim visiting these sites redolent of Methodist history will also be aware of the wider history of which the Methodist story forms a part: Warbstow Burrow (Iron Age fort), Chysauster (Romano-British courtyard houses), Roche Rock (medieval hermit's dwelling), Launceston Castle (where George Fox and St Cuthbert Mayne were both imprisoned), Tresillian (where the Parliamentarian commander, General Fairfax, received the surrender of the Royalist forces at the bridge), St Columb Major (where the Pretender was proclaimed King James III), and the Camel and Hayle estuaries where so many of the first Celtic missionaries arrived in Cornwall in the fifth and sixth centuries.

ACCESSIBILITY

A number of the places described in the Gazetteer are private property and their inclusion in the list does not mean that they are open for public viewing. At some of them visitors are welcome on occasion and at others not at all. The Gazetteer entries, where possible, will make the position clear. About 50 per cent of the parish churches named will be found open. For information about access to Methodist churches in Cornwall consult the District website www.methodistcornwall.org.uk. See also the Cornwall County site www.cornwall.gov.uk/history/ab-hi47.htm.

THE GAZETTEER

It is sometimes said that there are more saints in Cornwall than in heaven and for that reason the place names beginning with the prefix 'St' will be found, as has long been customary in Cornwall, arranged alphabetically under their own names and not grouped together under 'St'. So the following list begins with St Agnes.

The Gazetteer

ST AGNES

John Wesley visited St Agnes 17 times between 1747 and 1785. On one occasion he heard 'an excellent sermon' from the vicar, and on another 'two thundering sermons' from the curate. In 1760 Wesley reproved the members of the Methodist society for ceasing to attend church for Communion, and they promised him they 'would no longer give place to the devil'. The church which Wesley knew was, apart from the tower, rebuilt in 1848. On one occasion Wesley preached 'at the bottom of the hill' – presumably at Peterville. The old chapel at Goonown, in which he preached in 1785, is now a row of three houses in Goonown Lane. This chapel once had a floor of lime and ash, and a notice was displayed in the porch, 'Ladies, please remove your Pattens before coming into Chapel', as the iron rings on the wooden soles would cut up the floor.

The present church (1862), once a typical Victorian galleried chapel, was rearranged in 1964 with the help and encouragement of Captain Richard Waters. The church now occupies the upper portion of the building with the schoolroom beneath. On the side of the staircase is a polished wooden memorial board commemorating past members and office bearers of the period 1857-1948. In the schoolroom is a memorial tablet to the Revd Peter Parsons, minister of the church from 1857-60, and his wife Amelia who was a niece of John Opie, the portrait painter. This church, both for its setting and these special features, is worth a visit.

One of Cornwall's rare Methodist New Connexion chapels was built at Rosemundy, an area of St Agnes, in 1835, but it closed before Methodist union in 1932.

ALTARNUN

Over the doorway of the old chapel (1795, enlarged 1836) is a finely carved profile of John Wesley in Polyphant stone, one of the earliest works of the eminent sculptor, Nevil Northey Burnard, carved at the age of 18. Burnard's birthplace, marked by a plaque, adjoins the chapel.

Alturnun Church with the railed tomb of the Isbells on the right

The iron-railed tombstone of Digory and Elizabeth Isbell, Wesley's hosts (see Trewint) is on the right of the path leading to the church porch. The inscription describes the Isbells as Church Methodists, and reads:

Sacred to the memory of DIGORY ISBELL, who died in the Lord, 23rd

June, 1795 in the 77th year of his age. And of ELIZABETH his wife, who exchanged Earth for Heaven 8th October, 1805, in the 87th year of her Age. They were the first who entertained the Methodist Preachers in this County, and lived and died in that Connection, but strictly adhered to the Duties of the Established Church. Reader, may thy End be like theirs. From early Life, under the Guidance and Influence of divine Grace, They strengthened each other's Hands in God, uniting to bear their Redeemer's Cross and promote the interests of his Kingdom in the face of an opposing World, thus estimating Scriptural Christianity; in Youth, Health and Strength their Conduct was regulated by its Precepts; In Age, Infirmity and Death They were supported by its Consolations And in a happy Immortality They enjoy their rewards.

It is said that if you run 12 times round the tomb, and then put your fingers in your ears, you will hear the bells of heaven ring! On the bank opposite the church porch is the gravestone of Jonathan Harris (1853) which has a similar inscription. Another stone nearby is young Burnard's memorial to his grandparents, George and Elizabeth Burnard, who were members of the Methodist society. At the south-east corner of the church are memorials to the Nicolls family of Trerithick, a sixteenth-century farmhouse, who were hosts of John Wesley. Thomas Nicolls came to Trerithick with a young family around 1761. One of

the children, Edward (1758-1843), remembered Wesley laying his hand on him in blessing, presumably during Wesley's last visit to Altarnun in 1762.

ST AUSTELL

Wesley preached at St Austell 12 times between 1755 and 89 at two open-air sites in Fore Street and in the preaching house on West Hill. At the base of the church tower is the Mengu stone, a flat boundary stone which, in its original position at the entrance to Menacuddle Street, was the spot at which public announcements were made and where Wesley was known to have preached. Further up Fore Street he stayed with William Flamank (1742-1810) and preached from the front door steps of the house, presumably at 5 a.m. the following day. The house was probably at about numbers 15-21, opposite the HSBC Bank on the south side of the road. Flamank was a linen draper who seems to have had business contacts with another Methodist merchant, Richard Wood, Wesley's host at Port Isaac. Both men are mentioned in a Wesley letter of 1790 as being among his trusted supporters. A circuit plan of 1808, framed in the vestry at St John's, shows him as a local preacher, curiously described as a 'supernumerary'. Flamank's young daughter Elizabeth, (see Charlestown) once rode in Wesley's chaise to Port Isaac and remembered for the rest of her very long life that he had played 'peep-bo' with her in the carriage. The inscription on Flamank's tombstone (which can no longer be found) described him as 'a respectable merchant of this town, who raised himself to eminence by his own industry without neglecting his Eternal Interests' and added candidly 'being a stranger to disguise neither his frailties nor his virtues were concealed from observation'. A slab fixed to the wall to the west of the south porch of the parish church commemorates Flamank's first wife, Jane, who died in 1782. The inscription records, 'Her Funeral Text Rev Chap ye II verse ye 10'. A much-worn stone close to the wall on the right inside the cemetery gate in High Cross Street commemorates Flamank and his second wife, Mary. It is almost illegible but cannot have contained the missing inscription quoted above.

The schoolroom of the Baptist church on West Hill is substantially the chapel in which Wesley preached in 1787 (soon after it was built), and in 1789. In 1787 he attended a service at the parish church conducted by Parson Hugoe who had been the vicar for over 60 years, and later commented rather ungenerously, 'Oh what might a man full of faith and zeal have done for God in such a course of time.'

St John's Methodist Church was built in 1828, and restored and enlarged in 1892 by the architect Silvanus Trevail. Twenty-seven memorial windows were then added. These are of plain coloured glass except for the three centrally placed on three walls at gallery level – the gift of T.S. Grose. These are two-light windows. The one on the south side shows Christ the Good Shepherd and the Light of the World, and the one on the north has the figures of St John and St Matthew with their symbols. The entire front with its nine windows was rebuilt through the generosity of the Barratt family. The portico, brought to St Austell in 1828, was originally part of the short-lived Saunders Hill mansion at Padstow.

The central Barratt window consists of two lancets surmounted by a roundel containing a bust of John Wesley in the Romney style. Six further roundels spaced down the lancets are representations of the four evangelists with their symbols and the intertwined initials 'FB'. The inscription below states, 'In memory of Francis Barratt the father and Francis Barratt the son, the front of this chapel was restored and these nine windows were placed here by Francis Barratt the grandson and Anna Michell Barratt his mother, 1892.' The first Francis Barratt (1798-1873) had, it was claimed, an income of nearly £40,000 a year from iron mines in Cumberland. The second Francis (1831-81) had business interests at St Austell and Plymouth. The third Francis was Sir Francis-Layland Barratt, MP (1860-1933) who was High Sheriff of Cornwall in 1897. (See also St Blazey Gate.)

There are a number of memorials of historical interest in St John's.

Adam Clarke (1760-1832), a popular young preacher whom Wesley sent to Cornwall in 1784, had an outstanding ministry in east Cornwall and his work at St Austell was celebrated in the town a century afterwards. He later became one of the most distinguished of the Wesleyan presidents. Over the doorway on the left of the pulpit is a tablet which states that Richard

Glanville, 'the original lessee' of the premises, and George Michael, the architect of the chapel, were among his converts. A similar tablet over the doorway on the right records that Samuel Drew (1765-1833), the Cornish theologian, historian, local preacher and editor of *The Imperial Magazine*, joined the Methodists under the ministry of Adam Clarke. Another memorial to Drew, set up by public subscription, can be seen in the south aisle of the parish church.

Rather high up on the north wall at St John's is a marble memorial to the Revd Dr John Wesley Etheridge MA, Ph.D., a minister 'varied and mature in his Scholarship, learned in the Scriptures, impressive and powerful in the Pulpit'. Dr Etheridge was a Hebraist and seems to have been not a little eccentric, at times lapsing into Hebrew during his sermons! Mrs Reynalds, an experienced sermon taster, heard him at Truro and commented rather acidly, 'He would be better if he read less and prayed more.' At Penryn he accepted an invitation to preach for the Bible Christians, but objected when his name appeared on their noticeboard alongside that of a woman preacher! There are memorials to him not only at St Austell but also at Truro, Camborne and on his grave at Gulval.

Zion Methodist Church in Trevarthian Road closed in 1994. The schoolroom was the first Bible Christian chapel, opened by James Thorne on Good Friday 1828. The Bible Christian Conference met at St Austell, in the old chapel and the second one, on seven occasions between 1836 and 1904. Samuel Thorne 'Printer' (as he came to be called) and his wife Mary, 'The Maiden Preacher', lived at Mount Charles in 1872-73 and Samuel died there. Both are buried at Lake Chapel, Shebbear, in Devon.

Baldhu – see Billy Bray Country

Beeny – see Boscastle

ST BLAZEY GATE SX060537
Leek Seed Chapel (1826) got its unusual name because William Stephens, the treasurer at the time money was being raised for it to be built, was surprised by three young men as he was counting his money by candlelight. Feeling himself threatened he reached forward with a lighted taper in his hand towards a pile of leek seed. The intruders thought it was gunpowder and made a quick retreat. The inscription on his tombstone outside the chapel reads boldly: 'William Stephens, The Old Gardener, 1742-1822'.

Leek Seed Chapel

The chapel was completely renovated and reopened in 1904 through the generosity of Francis Layland-Barratt

MP in memory of his parents (see St Austell). In the chapel is a tablet to the memory of John (1774-1849) and Charity Williams of Bluegate, and their daughter, Margaret, the wife of Francis Barratt. 'They are removed from this house,' it reads, 'to the house not made with hands.' The chapel has a pleasing interior with a mahogany rostrum and fronted gallery. There is a round window with a portrait of John Wesley in the front of the building. To the left of the rostrum is a framed coloured picture on silk of Christ and the child in the midst and underneath it the three words 'St Blazey Gate' – evidently cut from the Sunday school banner.

William O'Bryan and his family lived for a time at St Blazey 'opposite the Duke William' and attended the old chapel, which stood on the site of the present one. It was in this building that he was expelled from the Wesleyan Society for the second, and last, time in 1815, before he made his way to north Cornwall and founded the Bible Christians (see William O'Bryan Country p. 70).

BODMIN
Wesley preached in the Guildhall on the south side of Fore Street, now number 20, a bakery and restaurant, and resplendent with a royal coat of arms on the exterior, in 1769 and 1774. The early Methodist preacher, Thomas Westell, spent some time in Bodmin gaol in 1744, having been committed there by the Penzance magistrates on a charge of vagrancy. In 1904 the Revd S. J. Finch, the Bible Christian minister at St Just, was imprisoned in the gaol (rebuilt c. 1855) for non-payment of rates in

protest against the Government's education levy. The gaol is now maintained as a tourist attraction. Wesley preached in the hamlet of St Lawrence in 1751 and must have seen the medieval buildings of the leper hospital which were still standing.

BODMIN MOOR
In 1743 Wesley described the moor as 'the first great pathless moor' beyond Launceston. He lost his way on that occasion but eventually reached Bodmin after hearing he 8 p.m. curfew bell ringing from the tower of Bodmin away to his left. It was not until 1759 that the turnpike road skirting the moor through Hallworthy and Camelford was constructed and not until ten years later that the direct route through Trewint and Temple was made.

BOLENOWE SW769379
A footstool said to have been used by John Wesley was preserved by the family of John Dennis who helped to build the chapel in 1892. 'Six Chimneys' on Bolenowe Carn was the birthplace of John Harris (1820-1884), the Methodist 'Miner Poet', whose work has recently been judged as 'a body of poetry as fine as any but that of half-a-dozen great poets of the Victorian age'. The former UMFC chapel closed in 1982 and is now a private house.

BOSCASTLE
The Methodist church with its entrance tower is halfway down the steep village street on the right. The first chapel was built by John Rosevear in 1801 as a thank-offering for the safe return of one of his trading vessels which had been

pursued by a French privateer. His son, Thomas Pope Rosevear, merchant, ship owner, quarry owner and Lloyds' Agent, rebuilt it in 1823-25. T.P. Rosevear later took the leading part in the reform movement which led to the decimation of the Wesleyan circuit in 1834-35 and introduced the Wesleyan Methodist Association to Cornwall. His portrait is framed in the vestry. The present church is basically the former Free Methodist chapel but fixed to the walls of the tower are the date-stones of 'Ebenezer, 1837' (the second Wesleyan chapel), 'Treworld 1838' and 'Siloam 1859' (Bible Christian chapels).

At Beeny (SX115925), a place associated with Thomas Hardy, the Bible Christians decided, in 1831, to extend their work to America in the wake of Cornish and Devonian migrant families.

BOTALLACK, St Just

The Manor House (1665) was the home of Stephen Ustick (1700-46), an active opponent of the first Methodists. Tradition says that he drove a pack of hounds through Charles Wesley's open-air congregation. This attractive house, now called Botallack Manor, was featured as 'Nampara' in the BBC-TV *Poldark* series. Bed and breakfast can be provided there today.

Botallack Manor House, 1665

BREAGE

On 5 September 1755, on his way from Helston to Newlyn, John Wesley called on W. Rowe in Breage. Rowe told Wesley of his conviction of sin 12 years before, which would have been during John's first visit to Cornwall. Although not intended Wesley opted to preach near Mr Rowe's home, and noted that 'The lions of Breage too are now changed to lambs.' The reference is unclear, for although Wesley refers to ten years previously, no mention of Breage is made in 1745.

The present chapel serving the village is the former Troon (Breage) Wesleyan chapel, now confusingly called Breaney, subsequent to the uniting of the societies at Breage and Sithney in 1991, and the closing of Sithney chapel. The former Wesleyan Breage chapel less than half a mile away, below the parish church, had been lost to the Wesleyans probably in the Wesleyan Association schism of 1835. It became a UMFC chapel in due course but closed in 1888. The old chapel became in succession the Parish Church Hall and then the Village Hall. Breage chapel is now a snooker and social club.

The former Bible Christian chapel on the north side of the green is now a private house called The Old Chapel. It closed in 1934 to join with Troon. The Breage BC Circuit was one of those strongly affected by the 1829 split between William O'Bryan and the main body of Bible Christians. The BC Circuit fell from 298 members to 41 by the secession of the Arminian Bible

Christians, but after their restoration in 1935 rose from 123 to 384.

ST BREWARD

In this granite countryside with Hantergantick Quarry close by, the former Bible Christian chapel (opened by James Thorne in 1871) and the present Methodist church (built in 1957 as a schoolroom following the wartime destruction of the old one) are both of local stone. The 1871 chapel was sold in 1985 and in the following year the 1957 schoolroom was converted into a triple purpose building to serve church and community.

BRIDGERULE

Before the boundary changes in the last century the parish of Bridgerule was divided by the Tamar, 'neither in Devon nor Cornwall' as Mark Guy Pearse described it 'but mostly betwixt the two'. At Lodgeworthy, on the Devon side, in 1815, William O'Bryan decided to proceed with the formation of the Bible Christians in 'the twenty or more parishes' in which his host told him there was no Methodist preaching. Close to the foot of the church tower is the broken gravestone of John Cory Cornish, one of O'Bryan's early itinerant preachers. Bridgerule is the 'Bridgestow' of Mark Guy Pearse.

BUDE

The first Methodist chapel was opened in Bude in about 1830, when a small house behind Garden Terrace was adapted for use. A slightly larger chapel near 'The Villa' was opened in 1835, but as the village developed into a holiday town larger accommodation was needed. Thus, under the guidance of the Revd Mark Guy Pearse, a site was selected on the south side of the river. The new building, in a Romanesque style, was opened in 1880. Since Methodist Union it has been known as Bude Central.

The town also boasts a Gothic revival chapel at Flexbury Park. Built by the UMFC and opened in 1905, it was said to have been designed by a local builder, John Pethick.

ST BURYAN

Wesley preached in the hamlet of Tredinney in 1747. In 1766 he attended a service at the church and afterwards preached from the hepping-stock (mounting-block) which can be seen by the church gate. According to a family tradition Wesley took the eight-year-old Constance Edmonds on his horse from St Buryan to Tavistock. More likely this would have been in 1782, when she was 12, and Wesley was travelling by chaise.

St Buryan Church showing 'Wesley's pulpit' on the right

After suffering extensive storm damage in 1979 the old chapel was demolished and the present one built in 1981. The schoolroom was added in 1984. The Bible Christian society here was originally part of the small Connexion established in west Cornwall by the former Wesleyan itinerant John Boyle in the early nineteenth century, which joined with the Bible Christians in 1817. The BC chapel closed in 1932 and was demolished in the late 1980s.

CALLINGTON
Pencrebar, on the right of the road to St Ives, was the home of the Rt. Hon. Isaac Foot, D.Litt., a leading Methodist and Liberal politician in Plymouth and east Cornwall. He was the Vice-President of the Methodist Conference in 1937 and father of several distinguished sons including Lord Caradon and the Rt. Hon. Michael Foot.

CAMBORNE
Both the Wesleys were welcomed by the Harris family, at what is now Lower Rosewarne, between 1743 and 1757. John Wesley preached near the church and also, according to tradition, by the elm tree at Knave-go-By which fell in a gale in 1974.

Wesley Chapel was built in 1828 in the 'London City Road style' after two members of the building committee had visited Bristol and Bath to examine the chapels there. The appearance of the interior, in which the Wesleyan Conference met in 1862, 1874, 1888 and 1903, was greatly altered by the introduction of the rostrum in 1911, and the pews were modernized in 1974. The proposal to remove the pulpit, replacing it with a rostrum, gave rise to many objections having regard to its historic associations, but these were met by embodying in the rostrum the mahogany fluted pillars of the pulpit. The rostrum was placed against a partition which then sealed off the apse, and the Communion area was brought forward to the front of the rostrum. The original sanctuary can be seen in the storeroom behind the rostrum. Similar alterations were made by the Victorians in many Cornish chapels of this style including Centenary Chapel (1839) at Camborne (rearranged 1939) where the apse, though denuded of its commandments table, is still intact.

Camborne Wesley has a number of memorials of interest, chief among them being Nevil Northey Burnard's bust of Dr George Smith of Trevu (1800-68). This tablet lists his academic achievements and publications and the fact that he was a magistrate but it does not mention his business activities as a founder of the Bickford-Smith safety-fuse factory or his directorship of the Cornwall Railway; neither does it quote Mark Guy Pearse's evocative description of his character as 'sunshine on granite'.

A marble tablet surmounted by a draped urn commemorates his close friend and contemporary Charles Thomas of Killivose (1795-1868) the founder of the fortunes of Dolcoath mine, class leader, local preacher, steward and trustee. Other memorials are to his son, Josiah Thomas (1833-1901), 'An eloquent man and mighty in the Scriptures', class leader, local preacher, trustee and, like his father, a mine captain at Dolcoath, and his grandson, Charles Vivian Thomas (1859-1941), local preacher, class leader and one 'who advanced every good cause'.

Other memorials commemorate Charles Edward Tyack of Trevu (1862-1931): 'To whatever work the Church called him he gave a ready and gracious response'; Thomas Vincent (1813-73) 'forty years an acceptable local preacher and class leader', and his son, Samuel, (1837-1910), Wesleyan minister; Samuel Stephens, (1839-1932) 70 years a member, during which he was a class leader, Sunday school superintendent, and trustee; Revd William Hill (1777-1814); Revd William Thomas Harris, MBE (1904-59) who served the Mende people in Sierra Leone from 1930-57; and Charlotte Philippa Boot (1839-98), youngest daughter of Sir George Smith. Also among the memorials is one to the Revd Dr John Wesley Etheridge (1804-66) that unusual man to whom tablets were also erected at St Austell and Truro (see also Gulval). The Camborne tablet says of him that 'his mind was well stored with various knowledge … he read and wrote several languages, was endowed with elegant taste, and possessed great ability in imparting instruction … above all he was an eminently holy man …'

Centenary Chapel, at the top of Trelowarren Street (mentioned above) was opened in 1839 to supplement the work at Wesley. Its chapel yard became the burying place of some of the leading families and benefactors of Camborne Methodism, particularly the Thomases, Smiths and Holmans.

Trelowarren Street Chapel was built in 1909 in New Connexion Street by the United Methodist Church, and was known locally as New Chapel. It was built following the closures of the earlier Bible Christian chapels in Rosewarne Road and Vyvyan Street. Its schoolroom was on the site of the Methodist New Connexion chapel (which was never widely represented in Cornwall), scene of the ministry of the Reformer Samuel Dunn, who had formerly been the Wesleyan Superintendent in Camborne and whose final memorial in Cornwall was to be the Wesley window in Truro Cathedral. Trelowarren Street Chapel closed in 1992.

North Parade Chapel, now closed and used as a store, was the United Methodist Free Church, but its schoolroom (recently demolished) was built by the Teetotal Methodists in 1842 (see St Ives). Trevu House, on Camborne Hill, was built as the Union workhouse and later converted into a residence by Dr George Smith; many Wesleyan events were held there. Redbrooke, further up the hill, was opened in 1879 as a Methodist secondary school for girls.

The Revd R. Hubert Luke, himself a Camborne man, was the Superintendent Minister of the Camborne Circuit (1955-62) and Chairman of the Cornwall District (1963-73). His wife, Pamela Luke, was Vice-President of the Methodist Conference (1982-83).

CAMELFORD
John Wesley visited Camelford frequently between 1746 and 1789, usually preaching in Fore Street by the market house. The town hall (1806),

now the library, stands on that site. It was in Fore Street that the young Humphrey Browning (1773-1864) heard him preach. The former Wesleyan chapel (1810) had become an Arts and Crafts Centre, but by 2004 was up for sale; its schoolroom is a dwelling house. The graveyard contained memorials of the early Camelford Methodists, notably of the family of the wool merchant Thomas Pearse (1758-1814), which included William and Mary Ivey who introduced Methodism to Holsworthy. The present Fore Street Church (built 1837 in early Gothic Revival style, and modernized inside in 1984) was opened by the Wesleyan Methodist Association shortly after the disruption of the circuit (see Boscastle). On the wall of the former Victoria Road Bible Christian Chapel is a tablet commemorating Samuel Pollard. It reads:

In the house adjoining this Church was
born one of Cornwall's greatest sons
Samuel Pollard
April 20th 1864 – September 15th 1915.
Bible Christian Methodist Minister
Missionary in China 1887 – 1915.
Pioneer Missionary among the Miao.
Mightily used of God.

The King's Arms Inn in Fore Street was used by both the Wesleyans and the Free Methodists for circuit meetings and committees. The reformers also used the town hall for services before the building of the Fore Street church.

CARBIS BAY
The church (1903) is a Gothic style building with a tower designed by Oliver Caldwell. Its windows commemorate,

among others, Captain Josiah Thomas of Camborne and his wife, one of them being 'raised by subscription from Dolcoath miners in memory of their late manager, Captain Josiah Thomas'.

CARFURY SW445341
This small community high on the Penwith Downs was close to the famous Ding Dong tin mine. John Bennetts, who worked underground at Ding Dong and was a member at Gear Wesleyan chapel, near Gulval, had begun a class meeting here in 1812. When Bennetts was disciplined in 1818 for teetotal convictions not favoured by the Gear leadership he left the Wesleyans and turned to the Bible Christians. The BC chapel consequently had a close association with the mine, with several mine captains among the members. The chapel was opened in 1832 and in 1843-4 a series of revival meetings saw many converted including miner William Rowe, who became President of the BC Conference in 1872. In 1866 a new chapel was built with the old one becoming the Sunday school. Declining population caused the closure of the chapel in 1970, although the memorials were transferred to High Street Chapel in Penzance. The building has become a private house. Carfury is the Racfury of Bible Christian minister John Osborne Keen's stories, notably his "Midst Mine and Moor and Cornish Folk".

There were also close links between Ding Dong mine and the Primitive Methodist society at Madron, that society going into decline from the closing of the mine.

CARHARRACK GWENNAP

Both the Wesleys preached many times in the mining parish of Gwennap. Most of their references to that parish appear to refer to Carharrack. The famous Pit was not mentioned until 1762. (See Gwennap Pit.) The site of the present Carharrack Methodist Church and its foreground seems to be the most likely spot where the Wesleys addressed great crowds in the 1740s and 50s. It would have been here that John Wesley was arrested, and then released, by Squire Beauchamp in 1745. A later preaching site was in a valley flanked by small hills, possibly along the lane which leads to Gwennap Pit. Wesley Chapel is on the site of Gwennap Octagon (1768) in which Wesley preached in 1775, and which it replaced in 1815. A local poet, writing in 1845, describes its early history:

A vast congregation Carharrack presents
On the Sabbath-day ev'ning, and
    former events
It recalls to the mind; here, too, the
    wise zeal
Of Wesley shone forth for the
    listener's weal;
The octagon chapel that was on this spot,
With his sanction first built, will soon
    be forgot;
Of those who there worshipp'd,
    not many survive.

Carharrack was the second Cornish chapel to be designed with an apse in the 'London City Road' style. It preserves its Victorian atmosphere with lamp-holders in position and 'free pews' so described. It has an unusual metal-plated ceiling. Today the church houses an extensive Museum of Cornish Methodism administered by the Cornish Methodist Historical Association. It is manned by volunteers at certain times during the summer months and can be opened to groups and individuals at other times by appointment; ask at Gwennap Pit. In the museum are displays relating to Wesley and his work in Cornwall, later Victorian Methodists, the United Methodists, the Primitive Methodists and the Bible Christians. There are stands relating to local preachers, Sunday school and choir, Cornish missionary work overseas, chapel china, Wesleyana, and individuals such as Billy Bray and Samuel Pollard.

CARN BREA SW685406

John Wesley climbed up the hill in 1770, having previously read about its antiquities (see Madron). He found 'the huge rocks strangely suspended one upon the other' and 'the rock basins' which can be seen close to the monument. William Clowes, the Primitive Methodist founder, was in Redruth in 1825. Feeling hungry he climbed Carn Brea but was able to find 'only one unripe blackberry'. The easiest access to the Carn by road is from Redruth to Carnkie where, at the end of the village, the lane to Carn Brea is signposted.

CAWSAND SX433502

In this unlikely village adjacent to Kingsand, the Bible Christians held their eighth Conference in 1826. There does not seem ever to have been a society here. (See also Kingsand.)

CHARLESTOWN SX037521

On the north side of the churchyard is the table-tomb of Edmund Shaw 'born in Yorkshire, January 21st 1767, died at Charlestown, May 18th 1863' and his wife Elizabeth, 1773-1872. Edmund was one of Wesley's travelling preachers and Elizabeth was the daughter of William Flamank, Wesley's host at St Austell. Their grandson, John Shaw, was the rector of South Hill and Callington from 1887-1906. The former Wesleyan chapel closed in 1998, and is owned by the Harbour Company. It has been used as a film set.

CHYNHALE SW641309

This attractive Gothic-style chapel in granite and Bath stone, unusual in West Cornwall, was planned by William Bickford-Smith of Trevarno in 1879, and was wholly or largely his gift. The Bickford-Smith vault is in the chapel yard. The architect was James Hicks of Redruth; the starred ceiling is unusual. Helston Folk Museum has on display the Wesley Guild Charter and the unusual 1935 Charter of Young Methodism from this chapel.

CHYSAUSTER SW473350

These Romano-British courtyard houses have been known locally as 'the chapels' because Methodists' gatherings were held there early in the nineteenth century. The Primitive Methodists seem to have used the site for some of their Camp Meetings, and possibly the Bible Christians also. It has been suggested that the stone slabs centrally placed in one of the rooms of 'House 3' were introduced to make a platform for the preacher.

ST CLEER

Samuel Pollard (see Camelford and Carharrack) attended the Sunday school at Hocking's House Bible Christian Chapel. The register showing his attendances is at the County Record Office, Truro.

ST COLUMB MAJOR

The former Wesley chapel on Fore Street (built 1868, rebuilt 1968) is now demolished and the space used as a car park. The former Congregational chapel is to the north of the car park, and on the south side is Messrs Edyvean's former printing works which became the Methodist church in 1980. This small building, which is outwardly unimpressive, has an interesting interior with oak panelling, Communion furnishings and pulpit. A reproduction on plate of the Chartres Last Supper is above the Communion table. The font is of De Lank granite and, like the Celtic cross in the window, in coloured acrylic, was made for the church. From 1974-80 a Methodist afternoon service was held in the parish church. The former Bible Christian chapel (1842), is almost opposite the car park in Fore Street. It is now part of Messrs Edyvean's printing works, and has an interesting 'early Gothic' frontage. Its date-stone carrying one of the famous 'BC' dates is no longer visible. Further down Fore Street to the south is the former UMFC chapel, now a youth centre.

COVERACK

This was the birthplace of the Wesleyan India missionary, J.T.F. Halligey. When Halligey left home to go to West Africa in 1870, his old class leader climbed the hill with him as far as Gate Wynyack, from where the horse bus left for Helston, and then on many Sunday mornings following the old man climbed to the same spot, knelt on the ground and said a prayer for the young missionary. The chapel closed in 1997, and the four framed boards, painted black, with white lettering, with the heading 'List of Services rendered by the Coverack Life Boat' covering the period 1902-77 were transferred to St Peter's Church. The chapel is now a private house. Coverack Bible Christian Chapel was affectionately called 'The Little Ship' and this building, which is now a thatched cottage facing the bay, still bears that name on a plate above the doorway. Over a second door is the inscription 'B.C. Chapel 1880-1935'.

The Little Ship

CUBERT

On the corner of the road to Crantock is the original chapel of c.1765, bequeathed to the Methodists in the will of Joseph Hosken (1698-1780) of Carines. It originally had a lime-ash floor and was furnished with rows of backless forms. Hosken added a wing to his house for the use of the preachers and had one of them in residence for a period. Wesley paid 12 visits to Cubert, often staying at Carines. He is said to have preached on the mound outside the garden gate, standing between two elm trees which are no longer there. Hosken's memorial tablet in the parish church is isolated from those of the rest of his family in the chancel, and curiously positioned high over the north aisle arcade (see also Bristol p. 72).

Cubert Chapel, c. 1765

CURY

Edward Boaden (1827-1913), a leading minister in the United Methodist Free Churches, and perhaps the main architect of the 1907 union of the United Methodist Free Churches, the Bible Christians and the Methodist New Connexion, was born at Treloskan in 1827. He was the President of the UMFC Assembly in 1871 and of the United Methodist Conference in 1907.

DELABOLE

Medrose is the one remaining chapel where once there were three. It was opened by James Thorne for the Bible Christians in 1863. Until the societies united in 1979, the former Wesleyan and Free Methodist chapels were at Pengelly, close to the entrance to the famous slate quarry which Wesley mentioned in his Journal in 1754 and may have visited when he was at Trewalder, q.v. Adam Clarke preached at the quarry in 1784-85 and a cavity on the eastern side used to be pointed out as 'Clarke's Hole', but development of the quarry has removed it. At Pengelly, during the disruption of 1835, a Mrs Skinner, who evidently sympathized with the Wesleyans, heated a poker at Nicholas Male's fireplace and then ran with it to the Wesleyan chapel and burned out the plug which the reformers had jammed into the keyhole! Nicholas' son, Matthew T. Male, served as a Wesleyan missionary in India from 1837-47 and 1858-66.

ST ENDELLION
A fifteenth-century church much loved by Sir John Betjeman, which Wesley (correctly for that period) called Port Isaac Church. He commended the society there for their regular attendance at the church although it was two miles away up the long steep hill. Here he heard 'an excellent sermon', in 1760, probably from the curate, William Buckingham. After the service he himself preached outside, 'a small distance from the church'. Endellion today has an established musical tradition. Note the bench ends, the Betjeman tablet, and the Ringers' Rhymes in the tower.

ST ERTH
A brass tablet in the north-west corner of the former Wesleyan church contains a tribute to the Revd Francis Tuckfield (1808-65) who worked among the Australian Aborigines from 1838-50 and became a champion of their rights.

It is not a memorial tablet but one that has a story to tell: 'On the 28th June 1849,' it records, 'the good ship "Larpent" arrived in Corio Bay from London having a fever on board. The late Rev Francis Tuckfield … visited the ship and saw the state of the passengers. As Good Samaritans he and his noble wife generously received a number of the sick into their home … At the 56th anniversary of their landing, the surviving passengers advised the erection of this tablet to record the Christly act – James Oddie, Benjamin Bonney, passengers, William Williams, pastor, 1906.' At the same time an identical tablet was placed in Yarra Street Methodist Church, Geelong, Victoria, New South Wales, where it can still be seen.

The Communion plate was given to the church in 1874 to mark the holding of the Wesleyan Conference at Camborne that year.

FALMOUTH
Wesley faced opposition on his first visit to the town in 1745. While he was in a house it was surrounded by a threatening mob and the door was broken down. Wesley stepped out into the street and faced the mob in his characteristic way, but his friends thought it best to smuggle him through a house that backed on to the riverside and sent him by boat to Penryn where he was later reunited with his horse. Neither of these houses can be identified but they would have been alongside the river in the present Church Street, Market Street or East Street. One house in East Street, known

to date from c. 1685, fits closely with the description which Wesley gives of both houses. In that house, a window looks across the Penryn river along which Wesley made his escape. He was probably a passenger in the boat but it is quite possible that he was at the oars. There is still a path by the riverside along which his opponents ran and shouted abuse at him.

On later visits to Falmouth Wesley preached near the church (1770) and in a preaching house and, according to local tradition, also on Golden Hill. In 1789 the aged Wesley preached 'on the smooth top of a hill', probably Pike's Hill above the church. In 1755 he found time to look around Henry VIII's Pendennis Castle. He thought that it could easily be strengthened, but considered 'our wooden castles are sufficient'.

The Methodist church on The Moor (reconstructed after war damage, in 1956) has, as its chief distinction, a Founders' Window, (John Hall & Sons, Bristol and London). On either side of the central figure of Christ, 'the Light of the World', are full-length portraits of John and Charles Wesley, flanked by medallions of Hugh Bourne and William Clowes (the Primitive Methodist founders), William O'Bryan, (the Bible Christian founder) and – the odd man out – Billy Bray. The side windows are of interest, particularly the one showing Christ in the boat with a sailor and a lifeboatman. The pulpit fall was the gift of Falmouth Parish Church. In the memorial chapel are tablets in memory of the Revd

Walter Pascoe Johns (1886), the Revd M. Wyche Mountford, District Chairman, (1915), and Mr and Mrs John S. McKinnon (1930).

John Harris of Bolenowe (q.v.), the miner-poet and Wesleyan local preacher, came to Falmouth in 1857 as Scripture Reader in charge of the Falmouth Town Mission, most probably one of the non-denominational missions being created at the time. A plaque attached to his second home in the town – 84 Killigrew Road – has the wrong date. There Harris died in 1884.

Pike's Hill Wesleyan Church was closed in 1979 and demolished but it is perhaps worth recording that the order of Morning Prayer was in use there from 1867-99. The United Reformed Church at Berkeley Vale is the former Bible Christian chapel, closed in 1956 when the society united with Wesley on The Moor. The Primitive Methodist chapel at Chapel Terrace had united with Berkeley Vale in 1939. Chapel Terrace is now a music studio.

'Langholme', the Methodist Home, in Arwenack Avenue, was opened in 1968. It now has 39 residents.

FOWEY
The King of Prussia Inn by the quay has an unexpected connection with Methodism. Its inn sign shows the Methodist smugglers, John and Harry Carter of Prussia Cove (see Rinsey). On the original form of the sign one side showed them on their way to the cove, and the other on their way to church carrying what appear to be Bibles or

Wesley's Hymns under their arms. The more recent sign simply shows two men in seamen's shirts and caps on one side, and two gentlemen on the other, one carrying what might be a book in what might be a bag.

Methodism no longer has a chapel in Fowey. The former Bible Christian chapel in Fore Street closed in 1948, when it joined with North Street ex-Wesleyan, the building becoming an Estate Agent, a shop and a house. North Street closed in 1977 when a united church was formed with the URC, but that in turn closed in 1993. North Street has been converted into flats.

FRADDON SW912579
William O'Bryan stayed overnight at the Blue Anchor Inn in 1836. He had emigrated to the USA in 1831, but was on one of his many return visits. His mother had died some time before and he was travelling in a cart with his mother's tombstone from Truro to the graveyard at Innis (see p. 70).

FROGWELL SX346685
The present chapel, 1864, succeeded an older one which, with an adjoining cottage and six acres of land, was left to the Methodists in 1802 by the will of Thomas Denner. Denner decreed that it was to be theirs so long as there should be three Methodists in Callington and Frogwell. He also left his four-poster bed with its curtains, sheets and pillows, for the use of the Methodist preachers 'and them alone'.

ST GENNYS
George Thomson, vicar of the parish for

50 years from 1732, has been called 'the first Cornish Methodist'. Several years before the arrival of the Wesleys he became an itinerant preacher and founded a number of religious societies along the coast of north Cornwall and north Devon. He visited them regularly in the course of what the rector of Marham Church described as his 'unwarranted circumforaneous vociferations'.

St Gennys Vicarage

During the 1740s he accompanied the Wesleys on their journeys into west Cornwall. Both John and Charles preached in his church on a number of occasions. Nearly 40 years later John Wesley was informed in Camelford that Parson Thomson was dying. He immediately rode to St Gennys and visited Thomson to whom he gave Communion, perhaps from the wine glass that is now at the Museum of Cornish Methodism (see Carharrack).

GODOLPHIN CROSS SW608313
The Methodist church (1934) was the first to be built in Cornwall after Methodist Union. The schoolroom was the Herland Cross Bible Christian Chapel of 1844 and on its wall is a stone tablet presented by the Bible

Christian Missionary Society, inscribed:

In loving memory of
JOHN CARTER
Who was born at Herland Cross on
December 17 1864
and died at Gan-King Training College
August 26 1890.
His honoured dust fills our first
missionary grave in China.

Below the tablet is a sheet of John Carter's sermon notes, now faded, but a transcript is also displayed. Other photographs make up the display. The Carters lived in the house (now called Road Side Cottage) next door to the chapel to the north.

GOLDSITHNEY
The present church opened in 1985, and is built on the site of its predecessor of 1841, the granite façade of which is to some extent reproduced in the present one (architect, Alan Percival, Falmouth). Wesley preached in the village in 1770, but the house called Wesley Cottage on the main street has no known connection with him.

There was a Teetotal Wesleyan Methodist chapel here, which passed to the Methodist New Connexion, and eventually to the Salvation Army before passing out of ecclesiastical use to become a builder's store. Its site is now the entrance to a modern housing estate.

GORRAN
Tregarton was the childhood home of Walter Lawry (1793-1859), missionary in New South Wales and the Friendly Islands between 1818-24, and General Superintendent of Wesleyan Missions in New Zealand and Visitor of the Missions in the Friendly and Fiji Islands, 1843-52. His father, Joseph Lawry, was the principal founder of Gorran High Lanes Chapel, which closed in 1977.

GRAMPOUND
The text board that stood on the wall behind the pulpit in the Bible Christian chapel here is now in the Museum of Cornish Methodism at Carharrack.

GRAMPOUND ROAD SW917504
The Wesleyan chapel was built in 1866 following the opening of the railway station. In 1984 the church became a partner in a Methodist-Anglican local ecumenical project, the first in Cornwall, although it no longer exists.

GULVAL
Both the Wesleys were at Gulval in 1744, visiting a society that already existed. John preached at Gulval Cross in the area now known as Trevarrack in 1747.

According to verses by Henry Quick, the eccentric Methodist poet of Zennor parish, on the death of John Uren of Boscrowan, spoken of Uren:

He did remember well
John Wesley preach at Gear,
how Christ
The lunatic did heal.

The first Methodist chapel in the parish was opened at Gear soon after the Great Revival of 1814, but has been long converted into a house. Its inclusion on several early nineteenth-century Plans as Gear Stamps indicates the close association of the early society with the tin streaming works in the adjacent stream. The first Wesleyan chapel at Trevarrack was opened in 1822. The building still stands on the west side of the hill about 25 yards up from the later chapel. Built to the designs of architect John Hicks, in an amphitheatre style, it was opened in 1884.

In the churchyard, by the path at the south-west corner of the tower, is the grave of the Revd John Wesley Etheridge (1804-66) and his beloved daughter, Eliza. The gravestone is marked with a cross, an uncommon feature on a Wesleyan memorial at that period. There are other memorials to the erudite and eccentric Dr Etheridge in St Austell (St John's), Camborne Wesley and Truro St Mary Clement churches.

In the south aisle of the parish church is a memorial to Philothea Perronet Thompson (1754-1823), who in her younger days had been one of John Wesley's young lady correspondents – his 'My dear Philly'. The imposing memorial records that Philothea was the wife of Thomas Thompson of Cottingham Castle, near Hull, the daughter of William Briggs Esq. of an ancient family in Norfolk, and a granddaughter of the Revd Vincent Perronet MA, vicar of Shoreham in Kent. She came to Penzance with her unmarried daughter in 1822 hoping that the climate would improve their health, but 'the two sick strangers' died within a few months of their arrival.

GWENNAP PIT SW718417

The preaching pit is signposted as 'Gwennap Pit' from Comford (Fox and Hounds) on the Falmouth to Redruth road, but do not be misled by the 'Gwennap' signs. At the entrance to Carharrack village turn left at the sign 'Gwennap Pit'. From the A30, travelling westwards, turn off at Scorrier and follow the signs to Falmouth as far as Carharrack where the Pit is signposted at the end of the village. Travelling eastwards from Penzance turn off at the sign 'Scorrier and Blackwater' and then, bearing left, follow the Falmouth signs as far as Carharrack, where Gwennap Pit is signposted at the end of the village. There is a brown sign on the A30.

The celebrated Pit was formed by the falling in of an old mine working in a district which is accustomed to such subsidences. It was first used by Wesley as a preaching place in 1762. He paid 18 visits to the Pit, always on Sunday afternoons, and addressed vast crowds of people, many of whom had travelled long distances to be there. His last visit was in 1789. In 1806 the Pit was remodelled, reduced in size and made more regular in shape as a memorial to John Wesley. An annual Whit Monday service was held there from 1807-1975, and was then transferred to the Spring Bank Holiday. The Pit consists of 12 circles of turfed seats decreasing in size from top to bottom. Various events and activities, musical, dramatic and social, take place in the Pit during the year and Sunday afternoon services are held throughout the summer.

The concrete and mosaic wall panels at the approach to the Pit were made by the sculptor and mosaicist, Guy Sanders, in 1983-85, to proclaim Wesley's message ('O let me commend my Saviour to you') to passers-by, to show the growth of Methodism throughout the world, and to tell the story of Gwennap Pit. In the small Busveal chapel, built in 1836, which adjoins the Pit, are framed prints of the Wesley family and of William O. Geller's highly imaginative painting of Wesley preaching at the Pit. The Visitor Centre, opened in 1988 by Mr John A. Vickers, was designed by Clive Buckingham, RIBA. It now forms an extension to the chapel with a coffee bar and sales desk.

GWITHIAN

Gwithian Chapel, 1810

Wesley rode through Gwithian in 1757 with Thomas (?) Harris of Rosewarne, Camborne, who showed him the place where his ancestors had lived before the encroaching sands finally buried the community of Connarton which lay around the road from Gwithian Bridge to the present village. An existing deed dated 1771 describes John Wesley as 'Protector of the Religious Society of the Parish of Gwithian'. The present

chapel, built in 1810, was the last thatched Methodist chapel in Cornwall. When the society ceased in 1995 the chapel passed to, and was rescued by, a private Trust, including Professor Charles Thomas, and under their auspices it is maintained and used for occasional worship.

By an old agreement visiting preachers had the right to stable their horses in the yard of the Pendarves Arms hotel, a reminder of the days when most preachers arrived on horseback or trap.

HAYLE

Hayle Methodist Church, 1972

Before the new 'causey' was built in 1825 travellers had to cross the Hayle river as best they could and a miscalculation could be dangerous. When Charles Wesley arrived in Cornwall in 1743, a few weeks in advance of his brother, he wrote, 'I passed the river Hayle just before the sea came in.' Many years later the aged John Wesley, travelling by chaise from Redruth, urged the young driver to make the crossing against his better judgement, and before they reached the shore the horses were swimming with the carriage in tow. Wesley called to him, 'Peter, fear not, thou shalt not sink.' When they reached St Ives, both of them were wet through, but Wesley saw Peter Martin and the horses safely lodged at the inn before making his way to the preaching house. Hugh Bourne, the Primitive Methodist founder, arrived at Hayle by steamer from Bristol in 1832 and walked to Redruth.

John Wesley preached at 'the Hayle' in 1765, and on two later occasions at Copperhouse where he met the society in its room, 'built with brazen slags'. That preaching house, the private property of the Cornish Copper Company, was followed by two nineteenth-century galleried chapels at Copperhouse and Foundry, as well as by the Free Methodist Mount Pleasant and the Bible Christian High Lanes chapels, all of which have given way to the present church, opened in 1972. Its principal feature is a range of 12 windows rising from floor to ceiling, each consisting of six-inch square glass blocks in which shades of red, green, yellow and gold predominate. The Communion table is in a recess flanked by a long gold-coloured curtain.

Heamoor – see Penzance

HELLESVEOR SW502398
A hamlet, a mile and a half from St Ives, on the Zennor road. The present chapel was built by the Wesleyans at Trezelah near Chysauster ancient village in 1905, and was brought stone by stone and re-erected here in 1937. The schoolroom is

the old Hellesveor chapel of 1844. In the corner of a field, near the junction of the roads to Halsetown and Towednack, is a stone from which Wesley is said to have preached. Three minutes' walk up the Towednack road can be seen, over the field hedge on the left-hand side, a massive rounded boulder. In Wesley's time there was a similar boulder over the hedge on the other side of the lane. The two together were known as Paal Maal, and a strong tradition points to the site as a Wesley preaching place, and describes the preacher's appearance and of his announcing the hymn on one occasion, 'All ye that pass by, to Jesus draw nigh'. Annual commemorative services were held at the Rock in the 1920s (see St Ives).

HELSTON
The Wesleyan chapel in Coinagehall Street was built by W.J. Winn in 1888. The schoolroom at the back of the present church, now known as the Epworth Hall, is the earlier Wesleyan chapel of 1794 (enlarged 1827) and has an apse characteristic of the period (see Carharrack). Here at Helston the apse is on the long wall of the building.

On the front of the building, curiously prominent, are foundation stones laid by the Secretary of the Conference, Mark Guy Pearse of the West London Mission, the Mayor of Helston and – a reminder of the Methodist stress on self-improvement as a concomitant of Christian holiness – a representative of the local 'Mutual Improvement Society'. The church has a fine moulded ceiling and a set of stained-glass windows illustrating Christ 'The Light of the World', 'The Teacher', 'The Good Shepherd' and the Ascension. Among the memorial tablets is one to George James Cunnack, Sunday school teacher and superintendent, class leader, circuit steward and missionary treasurer in the church, magistrate and honorary freeman of the Borough.

In 1988 the chapel was declared unsafe, and worship continued in the Epworth Hall until the refurbished chapel was opened in 1995. A fine and tasteful modernization has preserved all the windows and features, but has seen the old 'preaching auditorium' converted into a modern worship area at first-floor level, effectively filling in the balcony space, and providing meeting rooms below.

In Church Street the lower course of the former Free Methodist church (demolished 1969) can still be seen. A cartoon published anonymously in the town, c. 1911, indicates its former importance. It shows the devil standing outside the chapel and lamenting that he cannot follow his friends into the vestry where much of the town's business is being resolved! The former Bible Christian chapel still stands in the upper part of Meneage Street. The society had joined with Church Street in 1961. The building is now a squash and sports club.

In the Folk Museum in Church Street are two identical small Sunday school banners from Porthallow Bible Christian Chapel which used to be decorated with flowers and greenery for the annual procession, a copy of the Sunday school rules from Porthleven Bible Christian Chapel and copies of the Wesley Guild Charter and Charter of Young Methodism from Chynhale chapel. The table tomb of Samuel Drew (see St Austell) is in the parish churchyard near the west end of the church.

HICKS MILL SW766410

This Bible Christian chapel was built in 1821 and opened by William O'Bryan and James Thorne. It has since been enlarged twice. Hicks Mill was an important Bible Christian centre in mid-Cornwall and the Conference was held here in 1831, 1851, 1861 and 1871. Locally it came to be associated with its most famous member, Billy Bray, who joined the society in 1823 and later signed the total abstinence pledge in the chapel. One of the leaders of the society was Thomas Tregaskis (1785-1871), whose mill can be seen close to the chapel. He later moved to the Salt Water Mill at St Issey and was involved in a famous incident at Padstow (see Padstow). In the schoolroom there is a framed photograph of the members of the Bible Christian Conference at Exeter in 1865. James Thorne, in the centre of the front row, was the virtual second founder of the denomination.

ILLOGAN

Wesley preached to large crowds of tinners on Illogan Downs (assuming that the Three-cornered Down which he mentioned was, as seems likely, Illogan Downs). Charles Wesley was at Pool, which he described as being 'in the heart of the tinners', three times in

1743. He was moved on by the churchwarden as far as the boundary with Camborne parish. His opposers then went to the inn to celebrate which explains the curious entry in Illogan churchwardens' accounts for 1743 – 'Expenses at Ann Gatrell's on driving the Methodists … 9s 0d'. In Pool Wesley Chapel there is a reproduction in Mexican nickel of Da Vinci's *Last Supper*, a reminder of the nineteenth-century mining emigration. In the vestry is a Prayer Leaders' Plan dated 1850, notable for one of its rules, that leaders were not to spend longer time than was necessary in public houses.

The three successive chapels still standing on one site at Illogan Highway, built c.1809, 1839 and 1908, exemplify the growth of Methodism in the mining areas. The first stands behind the later buildings, and only its gable end can be seen from the road. It has long been the primary room, the second the schoolroom and the third the present church. On the outer wall of the schoolroom is a tablet, erected by Camborne-Redruth UDC, commemorating Thomas Merritt (1862-1908) 'once organist in this Chapel and composer of Christmas carols sung by Cornishmen and women the world over'. Merritt was also the organist at the nearby (now demolished) Chili Road Free Methodist Church. Another plaque to him can be seen at his birthplace in Broad Lane. The Merritt organ from Chili Road is now at St Andrew's Church, Pencoys. In Illogan churchyard are the graves of Thomas Merritt, Thomas Garland and Richard Hampton (see Porthtowan).

INDIAN QUEENS SW918587

Immanuel Chapel, now converted to flats as Chapel Court, was the former UMFC chapel; it closed in 1990. On the same side of the road, and accessible via Pocahontas Crescent about 150 yards to the north, is the Preaching Pit. Made from an old mineral working in 1850, it is an obvious imitation of Gwennap Pit, though it is larger and much wider at the base. In its early days it was described as Queens Sunday School Amphitheatre and was used by the various Methodist Sunday schools and others. It was renovated by local volunteers with help from the English China Clay Company (now Imerys) in 1976-78.

A little further down the road is the present, ex-Wesleyan chapel.

Innis – see William O'Bryan Country p. 70.

ISLES OF SCILLY

Wesley and two companions sailed from St Ives in the mayor's boat in 1743. Landing at St Mary's, he introduced himself to the Governor and presented him with a copy of the *Sherborne Mercury* newspaper and later preached outdoors. Wesleyan chapels were established on St Mary's at Old Town, Hugh Town and Holy Vale, closing in the 1930s, 1936 and 1955 respectively. The old Wesley chapel on St Mary's is said to have provided a direction marker for the captains of the *Scillonia* ferry boat. It became the town library, and Council Offices when the new library opened in 2004. The congregation at Wesley joined with the

Bible Christian congregation on the corner of Church Street and Well Cross in 1936.

The Bible Christians came to the islands in 1821 and established themselves with chapels on St Mary's, St Martin's and St Agnes, and had a meeting for a while on Tresco. The first chapel at Hugh Town was built in 1837 on the site now occupied by the museum. The Sunday school is now the parish church hall. In 1899 the new chapel, about a hundred yards further east, was opened. The St Martin's chapel dates from 1822 and was enlarged in 1837. A chapel was opened on St Agnes in the 1840s, and closed soon after 1932. It became the community hall, and occasional services were held until the early 1950s. The editor was pleased to be present on the next occasion a Methodist service was held on St Agnes, in the summer of 2003.

ST IVES

John Wesley's regular preaching place in St Ives was the Market Place, close to the parish church, and Charles Wesley preached there in 1743 amid much noisy opposition. John also preached in a number of unnamed meadows in and around the town, one of which may have been the Paal Maal site beyond Hellesveor Methodist Church. Other preaching sites mentioned by him were on the quay, on the cliff, and on a rock which jutted out four feet above the ground making a natural pulpit. According to tradition he also preached in Street-an-Garrow close to the entrance to Wesley Chapel. In 1743 he sailed from the harbour to the Scilly Isles.

The Wesleys were often seen in the parish church though the clergy in the early years preached against them. Charles, priest as he was, was refused Communion there on one occasion. John was at the church on a Public Fast Day in 1746, and in 1770 he listened to two 'useful' sermons. John Nance (1717-85), a builder and a host to both the Wesleys, 'ceiled the Trenwith aisle' (the Lady Chapel in the parish church) in 1751. He was churchwarden in 1768-70.

There was a building in St Ives in which a religious society was meeting before the Wesleys arrived in 1743, and a Methodist preaching house, perhaps on the Wesley chapel site, over the next 40 years. It was more than once extended or rebuilt but Wesley Chapel appears to be substantially the rebuilding of 1785. The roof was heightened and the windows altered probably during the alterations of 1825. There is no record of Wesley having preached in the building that we see today but it is highly likely that he did, and that he 'met the society' there.

Amid considerable controversy Wesley Chapel was closed in 1993, the society amalgamating with the adjacent Bedford Road society (see below). The building became a theatre workshop.

The chapel was built on a square plan and has a simple entrance doorway in Street-an-Garrow. A tablet by the side of this entrance is inscribed: 'Opposite this Chapel stood the house of John Nance at which John Wesley stayed during his earliest visits to St Ives in

1743'. An inner door in the church leading into the schoolroom was made during a mission led by the evangelist Thomas Cook, c.1890, to provide a convenient entrance into the inquiry room.

A block of old people's flats nearby has been administered by a trust associated with Wesley Chapel since 1905. A tablet on the building reads: 'In memory of John Thomas Matthews through whose generosity these buildings were erected'.

There were many miners but scarcely any fishermen in Wesley's society at St Ives, but Fore Street Chapel (1831), built by the Primitive Methodists, was for many years regarded as the fishermen's chapel. Primitive Methodism, never very strong in Cornwall, came to St Ives in 1829 (see Phillack) and quickly became established. One of its first meeting places was Quick's sail loft on the wharf, just beyond Mount Zion and above what is now the Friendship Restaurant and Trekenby Flats. In Fore Street Chapel are three framed charcoal drawings by W.H.Y. Titcombe, made in preparation for his paintings depicting Methodist life in St Ives a century ago. The paintings and their present locations are: 'Primitive Methodists at Prayer' (Dudley Art Gallery), 'A Mariner's Sunday School' (Doncaster Art Gallery) and 'Piloting her Home' (Toronto Art Gallery). A Camp Meeting, characteristic of the Primitive Methodists, was held on Borough Green, probably near the Island and in the vicinity of Borough Road, in 1829. Later Camp Meetings were held on Trencrom Hill two miles

south of Carbis Bay, near the former Prim chapel at Ninnis Bridge, now converted to a private house. The two-handled Loving Cup (or Love Feast Cup) from Fore Street is in the small museum at Trewint, q.v.

Bedford Road Church and schoolroom, together with the adjoining manse, were built by the Methodist New Connexion in 1900. Edward Hain of Treloyhan, the shipping magnate, was a generous subscriber to the building fund, and a stained glass window in the church is a memorial to his elder daughter, Grace (see Treloyhan Manor below). Teetotal Street in the town is a reminder that a Teetotal Methodist denomination was formed at St Ives in 1841. It reached as far east as Camborne but eventually joined the Free Methodist or, as in the case of St Ives, the New Connexion denominations (see Camborne and New Mill). A framed Teetotal Methodist circuit plan once hung in the vestry at Bedford Road.

The town museum on the wharf is said to have been a former Bible Christian chapel, but it is difficult to be sure about this. It contains little of Methodist interest except a small telescope unaccountably inscribed 'John Wesley'. The present 'Bible Christian' chapel is at the junction of St Peter Street and Back Road West. It was purchased from the Wesleyans in 1858 and extended in 1871.

Treloyhan Manor was built in 1892 for the shipping magnate Edward Hain, MP, Mayor of St Ives and Sheriff of Cornwall, the architect being Silvanus

Trevail who was responsible for many public buildings in Cornwall at that time. It is built of cut granite from the quarry at Castle-an-Dinas and yet has a surprisingly light and graceful appearance. The house, which became a Wesley Guild Holiday Home in 1948, still possesses some of its original furnishings. On the main staircase is a marble bust of Hain's 15-year-old daughter, Grace, who died in 1898 while still at school in London. The bust, of Florentinian marble, is signed, 'Fantacchiotti' (see Bedford Road above). In the dining room are A.W. Gay's three paintings of the Isbell Cottage at Trewint.

St Ives – see also Hellesveor.

ST JUST IN PENWITH

A mining town in which the development of Wesleyan Methodism can be studied in microcosm, from the first preaching to the building of the present Methodist church. Both John and Charles Wesley visited St Just as early as 1743 and attended services at the parish church which, as Charles Wesley noted in 1744, was crowded with the allegedly schismatical Methodists. Both the Wesleys preached by the cross at the entrance to the churchyard. John Wesley also preached in the market place and in the 'plen an gwary' where medieval miracle and mystery plays had been performed, and where the miracle plays ('The Ordinalia') have been performed again in the twenty-first century. Wesley stood on the wall which surrounds the enclosure.

On the bank on the right of the pathway near the south-east corner of the church is the tombstone of Jennifer Maddern, a Roman Catholic and a cousin of Walter and William Borlase (see Madron), who went to hear Wesley in the hope that the rumours that he was a secret member of her church and a supporter of the Pretender were true.

His host in the town was the innkeeper, William Chenhalls (1693-1780), whose house, with its three dormer windows, stands opposite the churchyard gate.

A silver crown piece (William III, 1696) which Wesley gave to his host's small son, also called William, for being a good boy at mealtimes, became a family heirloom and is now at the New Room, Bristol. Young William was probably the Royal Stannary Artillery Captain whose memorial is in the south aisle of the church.

William Chenhalls' Inn

Chenhalls' house would have been the first home of the Methodist society in the town, but the house in North Row, now called 'The Meeting Place' was already in use as a Methodist society house when Charles Wesley was there in 1746 and it continued to serve the society for class meetings and weekday preaching services until 1755. On Sundays the society members attended the parish church, as they did at Altarnun and many other places. Although The Meeting Place is not in Methodist ownership and is not open to the public it has in recent years been occupied by a Methodist, and the present editor has had many a cup of coffee there!

'The Old Sunday School' in Cape Cornwall Street is a private house. The older part of this building replaced the society house in North Row in 1755. Wesley preached from its foundation stone on 13 September, when he described it as the 'new society house'. When he returned to preach there two years later he thought it to be 'the largest and most commodious in the county'. In 1799 it was extended towards the town, the new part becoming the Wesleyan chapel and the old part the schoolroom. After 1833, when the present Methodist church was opened, the Cape Cornwall Street property became the schoolroom, and is now known as 'The Old Schoolroom'.

The Society House

The present Methodist church (1833), at the end of Chapel Street, still dominates the town. It is said to have been a landmark for sailors and the last building in Cornwall that many emigrants from north Cornish ports saw as they sailed out into the Atlantic in the last century. In the chapel is a memorial to 20 miners who were drowned at Wheal Owls mine in 1893 when they holed into flooded workings. The Ionic pillars of the rostrum, introduced in 1893, appear to have been part of the original small pulpit which would have stood in front of the Communion area.

In 1744 Charles Wesley and John Meriton, a clergyman from the Isle of Man, took some time off for recreation and, as Wesley later recorded, 'I climbed up and down Cape Cornwall with my brother Meriton, to the needless hazard of our necks.'

The Bible Christians had a chapel in Bosorne Street, now demolished, and on Bosorne Terrace is St Just Free Church, the sole surviving Wesleyan Reform Union chapel in Cornwall (see Liskeard). Its origins lie with the Wesleyan Reformers of the 1850s, but drew strength from various local separations from the Wesleyans.

KEHELLAND SW622410
The present chapel was the former Wesleyan Lower Chapel. It has been modernized and a link put through to connect the 1891 chapel with the 1850 building alongside. On the outer wall of the chapel is a metal bas-relief of the head of John Wesley by Rosalind Danecourt, dated May 3, 1956. The

former UMFC Higher Chapel was closed in 1957, and the site is now houses.

KENNEGGY DOWNS SW480330
Charles Wesley preached to the tinners here three times, and John Wesley once, in 1743. In the vestry of the ex-Wesleyan Kenneggy chapel (1842, but much modified internally) hangs a copy of the 1829 Hayle circuit plan covering 15 Sundays from 17 May to 23 August.

Kerley Downs – see Billy Bray Country

ST KEVERNE
The birthplace of William Jenkin (1757-1844), an early Wesleyan missionary to the West Indies. As a boy, he was present in St Keverne Church on the day in 1770 when lightning struck the spire and damaged the building. Lanarth was the residence of Lt. Col. William Sandys of the Indian Army. A churchman sympathetic to the Methodists, he addressed the Wesleyan Conference and gave helpful advice to Thomas Coke when he was preparing to take Methodism to India. He dined with Coke at Helston, probably at the Angel Inn. The present schoolroom was opened by Kenneth Kendall, a television newsreader, in 1971.

KILKHAMPTON
The churchyard is the scene of James Hervey's once classic but now hardly known *Meditations Among the Tombs*. Hervey was a member of Wesley's Holy Club at Oxford. William O'Bryan and his family lived at Undertown from 1816-19.

KINGSAND
The chapel, now closed, used to have on the wall a painted board showing the Royal Arms. Common enough in parish churches, it was an unusual feature in a Methodist chapel, rather surprisingly, for in many places in the country the Wesleyans expressed their loyalty to the monarchy by calling their chapels Hanover and Brunswick. See also Cawsand.

LANDRAKE
It was announced early in 2005 that the old church and schoolroom is to be sold for housing and a new church is to be built on land at the back of the property.

LAND'S END
In 1743 and 1757 John Wesley stood at Land's End and reflected, 'I know no [other] natural curiosity like this.' In 1785, at the age of 82, he again 'clambered down the rocks to the very edge of the water' thinking it likely that the sea had gained a hundred yards since his first visit. In 1743 Charles Wesley and a companion also walked 'to the extremist point of the rocks' and sang verses which he had just composed:

Come, Divine Immanuel, come,
Take Possession of thy Home,
Now thy Mercy's Wings expand,
Stretch throughout the happy Land.

Carry on thy Victory,
Spread thy Rule from Sea to Sea,
Reconvert the ransom'd race:
Save us, save us, LORD, by grace.

When the Revd William Driffield was the Primitive Methodist minister at St Ives in 1837 he visited Lands End and '... the Logan Rock, [and] called at the first and last Inn in England. Mr Richard Brotheras sang and prayed on the rock, where Wesley composed that hymn, "Lo on a narrow neck of land, etc." ...' The quotation is of the second verse of the hymn 'Thou God of glorious majesty', number 61 in the Primitive Methodist Large Hymn Book of 1825, number 58 in the Wesleys' 1780 book, and its ascription to Lands End is erroneous; the words but recently composed in 1743 are those quoted above.

The modern entertainment complex at Land's End has a permanent exhibition called 'The Spirit of Cornwall' in which John Wesley, Gwennap Pit and Billy Bray have a modest place.

LANDULPH
The chapel organ was formerly at All Saints, Brixham, where Henry F. Lyte, the writer of 'Abide with me', was the perpetual curate. The organ came to Landulph in 1934.

LANEAST
The church has been little altered since the Wesleys preached from its sixteenth-century pulpit a number of times between 1744 and 1750. In the north aisle is a memorial to John Couch Adams, the astronomer (see Tregeare and Truro Cathedral).

LANHYDROCK (National Trust)
The museum collection contains four trowels presented to members of the Agar-Robartes family at Methodist stonelayings.

LANSALLOS
The Wesleyan Association Burial Ground at Mabel Barrow contains the memorial obelisk of Dr Jonathan Couch (1789-1870), doctor, naturalist, local leader of the Wesleyan Methodist Association and grandfather of 'Q' (Sir Arthur Quiller Couch). On the wall at the entrance to the burial ground is a slate tablet inscribed 'Ebenezer Chapel and General Burying Ground 1851'.

LAUNCELLS
William O'Bryan enrolled the first recorded Bible Christian membership at Shernick farmhouse (SS 275048) on 3 October 1815, two days after making the decision to separate from the Wesleyans.

LAUNCESTON
Wesley preached on St Stephens Down on his way out of Cornwall in 1747, and again in 1748 and 1750. His comment on his hearers in 1748 was that as soon as he had finished speaking 'surely never was such a cackling made on the banks of Cayster'. The site is now the golf course at St Stephens. Wesley stopped in the town for the first time in 1751 and a mob gathered round the house while he was speaking. It is thought that this house was on the site now occupied by 18 Church Street, just after High Street joins, now occupied by Castle Jewellers. He attended service at St Mary Magdalene that year. In the following years he usually preached in the town hall in the square before meeting the members of the society.

On one occasion, he met 'the stewards of all the East Cornwall societies' in 'a nearby room'. The location of his preaching place in 1755 – a remarkable 'gentleman's dining room capable of seating some hundreds of people' – is not known, though Madford House has been suggested, and so has Tregaeare House six miles away in Egloskerry parish.

The present Methodist church, of 1870, is the third on the site close to the castle. It is one of the few Cornish Methodist churches built in the Gothic Revival style with nave, chancel with narrow apse, tower and spire, mainly of Bath stone and granite. The pulpit and font are of Bath stone. The architects were Hine and Norman of Plymouth. The Bath stone in the tower did not prove durable, and the spire, which from 1870-1984 made a distinctive contribution to the Launceston skyline, had to be taken down. In the vestry is a framed plan of the Launceston Circuit, 1848, and an oil painting by J.L. Pethybridge of the near-centenarian local preacher William Browning (1797-1896), a son of the Humphrey Browning who heard Wesley preach in the street at Camelford, and the grandfather of Alfred Browning Lyne, who was the proprietor and editor of the *Bodmin Guardian*. In the adjoining Institute (1891) is a memorial window to John Dingley, JP 'for nineteen years President of the Men's Bible Class'.

Launceston College, now the comprehensive school at the top of Windmill Hill, was founded (as Dunheved College) by a group of Wesleyan Methodists, and opened by the President of the Wesleyan Conference in 1873. The Wesleyan burial ground at the bottom of St Thomas' Hill, in use from 1822-1945, contains memorials to the Dingles, Pethybridges and other leading Methodist families. In the collection of the Lawrence House Museum in Castle Street are several mock figures of John Wesley made from ox's vertebrae. Books in the museum collection include an uncommon edition of the Bible bound with the 1831 version of 'Wesley's Hymns'.

Badash House, then in the countryside on the South Petherwin side of the town, was rented for a few years by William O'Bryan and the first two Bible Christian Conferences (1819 and 1820) were held in the house. Its location was in the region of the modern Health Centre on Landlake Road, but it no longer stands. Catherine O'Bryan not only fed the preachers but celebrated the occasion in verse:

*The year one thousand and eight
    hundred and nineteen
In the Borow Dunheved some
    preachers were seen,
Twelve brethren there met for
    spiritual talk,
How Christians should think and
    how they should walk.*

In this verse 'Borow' represents the local pronunciation of 'Borough', Dunheved being the ancient name of Launceston.

From Badash Mary O' Bryan (1807-83)

walked to school in Castle Street, passing the castle gateway where, on one occasion, she saw 'two men hanging'. From Badash the family moved to Race Hill and later to Dutson about a mile north west of the town on the Holsworthy road. The later Bible Christian chapel in the town was on Tower Street. Opened in 1851 it became the Sunday school when a new chapel was opened adjacent down the hill in 1897. That in turn was demolished in 1982, the society having amalgamated with the ex-Wesleyan society at Castle Street in 1974. The original chapel is now converted into flats.

The UMFC chapel on St Thomas Road had been opened by the Wesleyan Methodist Association in 1840. It closed in 1946, became a brush factory in 1947 and was demolished in 1998.

St Cuthbert Mayne, the Roman Catholic martyr, and George Fox, the Quaker, were both imprisoned in the castle gaol.

LELANT DOWNS
A National Trust marker on the right-hand side of the upper road from Hayle to St Ives (SW524368) inscribed 'The Bowl Rock' draws attention to the large rounded granite boulder lying in the bed of a stream. 'The Bowl Rock' or 'The Giant's Marble' is said to have been used by the legendary giants of Trencrom Hill. One of their children dropped the marble and it rolled down to its present position. According to tradition Wesley addressed a hostile crowd at this site, and cursed one man in particular, saying, 'Old man! Thou and all thy name in this place shall be blotted out from under heaven.' Absurd as this sounds, there are passages in Wesley's published Journal which partly explain how such a story could get into circulation. Across the road the former, once thatched, Bowl Rock Chapel is now a house.

LISKEARD
On several occasions John Wesley passed through the town on his way to the Tamar crossings at Saltash and Torpoint. He preached on the Parade in the centre of the town in 1757, taking his stand at the Bull Stone to which the bulls had been tethered and which is now in Castle Park.

(From the Parade, Castle Park can be reached by proceeding along the road marked successively Pike Street, Market Street and Castle Hill, and then crossing Castle Street into a lane which bends to the left.) The Bull Stone is close to the park entrance, set in a small flower-bed. Wesley preached in the town hall, built over the ancient Pipe Well, in 1775. The well, though not the town hall, can be seen in Well Lane. Number 18, Castle Street, a white-painted building inside the gate to Church Park House, opposite the parish church, is now known as 'Seal Hayne' but it is basically the 1776 Wesleyan chapel, with preacher's stable underneath, in which Wesley probably preached when he was in the town in 1787. The original stone walls can be seen from the south side.

The present Wesley Chapel was built in 1846 to replace a slightly earlier one of 1841 which had been destroyed by fire.

A framed drawing of the older chapel can be seen in the vestry. Under the Communion table is a stool bearing a brass plate on which is inscribed – 'On this stool the Rev John Wesley, MA stood when preaching at St Winnows (St Twindles), a hamlet near St Germans in the home of Mrs Ann Charlick in 1775 and in 1785 … presented to the trustees, for use in the rostrum, by James E. Moon … 1909'. A letter from Mr Moon, giving fuller details, is framed in the vestry.

There are stained glass windows, of Christ blessing the children (in memory of Henry and Amelia Lucas, 1882) and Christ the Good Shepherd commemorating S.J.P. Sowden who died at Bloemfontein, South Africa, in 1898. On the rostrum, made by the local carpenter and craftsman John Ugalde in 1889 to replace the pulpit, can be seen the fleur-de-lys, the emblem of the Borough of Liskeard, and this motif can also be seen in other places around the church.

In the schoolroom are two wall tablets, one of which reads: 'In commemoration of the Revd Thomas Coke, LL. D. founder of the school in 1803. What hath God wrought!' Dr Coke, often described as the Founder of Methodist Missions Overseas, was also an early advocate of Home Missions and of Sunday schools. He visited Cornwall in 1803 advocating the formation of Sunday schools. The other tablet commemorates 'The Rev William Beal, the first teacher', a native of Liskeard, who was a Wesleyan minister from 1808-72.

The Bible Christians came to the area in 1817, their first expansion into Cornwall from the area around Holsworthy (see Launcells). Their first meeting place in the town was at a house in Lower Lux Street, demolished in 1965. When the Arminian Bible Christians separated with William O'Bryan in 1829 (see Breage) the Liskeard society went with him; O'Bryan lived in the town from 1828 until he emigrated to the United States in 1831. Later the Bible Christians used the Temperance Hall, and in 1854 built a chapel in Lamellion Street, now called Russell Street. In 1924 this chapel closed in favour of one United Methodist Church society at Greenbank and was sold to the Wesleyan Reformers (see below). Sam Pollard senior, father of the China missionary (see Camelford) was three times a minister in the Liskeard Circuit, and is buried in Station Road cemetery.

When the Wesleyan Methodist Association separated from the Wesleyans (see Boscastle) Liskeard Methodists joined the schism, and a WMA circuit was established for Liskeard and Looe in 1837. The society in the town first met in the Market House, but a 'shareholder chapel' was opened on Greenbank in 1838. The WMA circuit became part of the United Methodist Free Churches in 1857, and, although by then there was a circuit of Wesleyan Reformers based in the town, albeit without a town chapel, they declined to join the UMFC. The UMFC chapel became the Greenbank United Methodist chapel in 1907, and closed in 1997 as a Methodist Chapel, the society amalgamating with Wesley. The building became a Pentecostal Church Centre.

The Wesleyan Reformers arose on the wave of democratic reform that was characteristic of the late 1840s, the 'Fly Leaf controversy' in the Wesleyan Conference, and the autocracy of that Conference, which led to expulsions and secessions. By 1857 there was a Reform circuit in the Liskeard area, but without a chapel in the town. This circuit declined to enter the UMFC in 1857, and, along with similar circuits and chapels across the country, became part of the Wesleyan Reform Union in 1859. They acquired a town chapel in 1924 when they purchased the former Bible Christian chapel in Russell Street. In 1959 the Reform circuit was very isolated from a Connexion which had its headquarters in Sheffield, and its strength in the north Midlands-south Yorkshire area, and amalgamated with the Methodist circuit. Russell Street closed almost immediately. The chapel, which had then been in four Methodist denominations, became the home of the town Silver Band, a service it still performs.

The fifth Methodist denomination to have a presence in this small town was Primitive Methodism. After a few attempts at starting, the town appeared as a mission station in 1856. The Primitive Methodists might also have had an early meeting place on Russell Street. In 1868 a property in Pound Street was sold to them by the Borough Council, and in 1871 they built a new chapel on Castle Hill, now the Seventh

Day Adventist Church. The circuit always struggled, and it was wound up in 1924. Castle Hill was put up for sale, and viewed by the Reformers, but Russell Street was chosen, and it was there that the few remaining Liskeard Primitive Methodists seem to have gone.

THE LIZARD
The early travelling preacher, Richard Treffry, who became President of the Conference in 1833 and who was in the Helston Circuit in 1800-02, records on one page of his journal: '5 May 1802 … Lizard … Walking on the cliff in the afternoon saw a smuggler land his goods, but in consequence of this we had very few hearers.'

LOOE
Riverside Church on the quay at West Looe was built as a Congregational church in 1880 in succession to an earlier one, built in 1777 by the Revd Sir Harry Trelawny (see Wadebridge). In 1966 Riverside became a joint Methodist and United Reformed Church – the first in Cornwall. In 2003 the East Looe congregation joined the union.

The former Wesleyan chapel in Shutta Road in East Looe is now 'The Old Hall Bookshop'. It was replaced by the Barbican Methodist Church which was opened in 1968 as a modern dual-purpose church and community centre, but closed in 2003.

LOSTWITHIEL
John Wesley must have passed through the ancient Duchy capital on at least three occasions between St

Austell and Liskeard, to and from the Tamar crossings at Torpoint and Saltash, but generally he preferred the old high road between Launceston and Bodmin. He never mentions the town, and does not appear ever to have stopped there. The origins of Methodism remain obscure.

The imposing former Bank Chapel on Queen Street was opened by the United Methodist Free Churches in 1900, as the inscription reveals. It closed in 1987, and is now flats. The former Wesley chapel had been on part of Restormel Road now occupied by the modern A390, Liddicoat Road. The actual site corresponds partially with the Talbot Hotel car park. The congregation joined Bank in 1961. Since 1992 the society have occupied their own building near the library.

LUXULYAN
Medrose is a sixteenth-century farmhouse, where Wesley stayed with the Pascoes, and in which he held the East Cornwall Quarterly Meeting in 1765 and 1768. It was here that Thomasine Lawry, the mother of William O'Bryan, envied the servants who had the privilege of cleaning the preacher's boots. The house is strictly private. Gunwen Farm was the birthplace of William O'Bryan, the Bible Christian founder (see William O'Bryan Country p. 70).

MADRON
Until 1871 the parish included Penzance. In 1744 Wesley preached on Tregavara Downs, near the north-pointing arm of the modern Drift Reservoir. Walter Borlase, the vicar of the parish from 1720-76, was a clerical magistrate and a vigorous opponent of the Wesleys in West Cornwall in 1744-45. The leaders of the Methodist societies were viewed with suspicion by the magistrates and others who suspected them of being Jacobite agents at a time when there was a real danger of a French invasion of the Cornish coast. Walter Borlase has often been confused with his brother William, the antiquary and naturalist whose book, *The Antiquities of Cornwall*, was published in 1754. Wesley read it while he was in the county in 1757 and commented, 'He is a fine writer, and quite a master of his subject ...'; a compliment that Dr Borlase could hardly have returned for he had already described Wesley, in a letter to the bishop, as 'this quack'.

The present Methodist chapel was opened in 1903, in spite of the previously engraved date-stone, which reads 1902. A Wesleyan chapel, it replaced the small 1800 chapel immediately opposite it, a location now covered by bungalows.

Old Chapel House, opposite the cemetery, stands on the site of the Primitive Methodist chapel opened about 1847. The society was strongly dependent upon the fortunes of Ding Dong mine higher up on the moor (see also Carfury), and in 1867 John Dunn, a twenty-year-old local preacher and prayer leader at the chapel, was killed in a surface accident at the mine. When Ding Dong closed in 1879 the Primitive Methodist support declined, with the

Cock family keeping it going. When Warwick Cock died in 1916, with his son away on war service, there was no energy left, and the chapel closed. The few remaining Primitives joined the Wesleyans.

MANACCAN
Richard Polwhele, the historian, antiquary and literary opponent of Methodism, occupied his 'snug little vicarage' at Manaccan from 1794-1821. He did not appreciate the early Methodist preacher who took his stand and preached close to the vicarage wall! Charles Tresidder (1846-1926), whose woodcuts can be seen in *Daniel Quorm* and other books by Mark Guy Pearse, was a Manaccan man. The mounting stock stands outside the Methodist schoolroom which has replaced the chapel of 1835.

MARAZION
Wesley came here with the vicar of St Gennys in 1745 to attend a meeting of the justices who had arrested one of his preachers as 'an able-bodied man without lawful calling or sufficient maintenance'. During his long wait for the case to be heard Wesley climbed up St Michael's Mount and saw the 'large and pleasant' house, but he could not forbear commenting afterwards that Sir John St Aubyn had repaired and beautified the apartments – and then died. In 1789, on his last visit to Cornwall, the 86-year-old Wesley preached 'a short sermon' in the new preaching house at Marazion.

From the late eighteenth century there was a Wesleyan society on the Mount,

and the 1851 census dates a chapel to 1820. This is said to have been located 'where the ticket office is now'. By 1877 the society had ceased and had become part of Marazion.

The former United Methodist Free Church chapel on West End closed in 1965 and is now a St Aubyn Estate workshop. Curiously Joseph Thomas (1840-94), a UMFC local preacher and a worshipper at this chapel, had been assistant Estate Agent and lived on the Mount.

The UMFC chapel has been wrongly identified in a local publication as the former Bible Christian chapel; that chapel was on one of the back streets. It closed before the First World War. The present chapel on Fore Street was opened by the Wesleyans in 1893.

ST MAWES
The present Roman Catholic church was a Bible Christian chapel from 1875-1937. At the suggestion of Canon A.P. Chapple, the priest-in-charge, the centenary of the building was celebrated, in 1975, at a service in which the Methodist Superintendent, the District Chairman and the Rector of the parish took part. A framed chronology in the porch outlines this church's unusual history.

The former Wesleyan chapel (1816) closed in 1997.

ST MAWGAN IN PYDAR
The former Mawgan Cross chapel was built by the Wesleyan Reformers and later taken over by the Bible Christians. During the war the RAF station

gradually surrounded it until, in 1944, the trustees received a letter from the Air Ministry saying that the chapel had to come down for it would be 'a flying obstruction on the runway'.

MEVAGISSEY

Wesley visited Mevagissey in 1753 and preached at a house a mile from the town, most probably Trewinney, the home of James and Mary Lelean. According to tradition they had protected him from the mob and as a mark of his appreciation Wesley gave his silver shoe-buckles to Mary Lelean. The buckles were later in the possession of Dr W.E. Orchard, a Congregational minister who later became a Roman Catholic priest and who wore them when he said mass. Later they were owned by an Anglican priest and today are in the Museum of Methodism at City Road Chapel, London. Nicholas Lelean of Trewinney, the master of the *Seven Sisters* schooner, was for nine years a prisoner of the French revolutionaries. He and his wife, Catherine, were members of the Methodist society in the town: their tombstone can be seen in the churchyard close to Trewinney.

Wesley is said to have been entertained at the three-storied building on the east side of Market Square which is now a shop called 'Ocean Pearl'. He was a friend of the Dunn family and probably also stayed at their house, now The Haven Restaurant in Fore Street – see the painting in the town museum. Captain James Dunn, known as 'the old Reprobate' and his son of the same name, also a sea captain, were influential men and smugglers, though

James Jnr. gave up the occupation when he became a Methodist in 1805. Wesley disapproved of smuggling because it involved 'cheating the King'. In the next generation the captain's son, Samuel Dunn (1798-1882), became a leader of the Methodist Reformers throughout the country (see Camborne and Truro (Cathedral)). The Wheel House Restaurant on the West Wharf was the first Wesleyan chapel in the town (1757); its top storey has been removed.

Both the Wesleyan chapel and the Bible Christian chapels are now flats, the ex-Wesleyan in Fore Street closing in 1966 to join with the ex-Bible Christian chapel in River Street, but that closed in 1992 to join with the URC chapel in Chapel Street.

St Michael's Mount – see Marazion.

MITCHELL

Plume of Feathers Inn, Mitchell

The Plume of Feathers Inn was a stopping place for the Wesleys on their early visits to Cornwall. But John Wesley suspected that Mrs Morgan, the innkeeper's wife, had been spreading scandalous stories about him, though she denied it when Wesley later confronted her. Before the village was by-passed by the modern A30 the attractive portico at the front of the inn had twice been demolished by runaway lorries and built again.

MORVAH

Wesley preached at Morvah on many occasions: at Trevowan, at Rosemergy, on the north side of the church, on the lee side of a house and on sloping ground where 'the congregation stood rank upon rank as in a theatre'. John Nelson, Wesley's companion in 1743, attended a service at the church. Of that building, only the tower remains. The former Wesleyan chapel, on the inside of the lane round the bend from the church, is now a house. Adjoining this building, close to the bend in the lane, and set at an angle to the roadway, is the original society house. Once a one-storey building it has recently been heightened. There were 150 members in the society here in 1744 when Charles Wesley prayed at the site while it was being built.

The former chapels

The hamlet gave its name to the original Bible Christian circuit in the west, and was part of the Boylite Circuit absorbed in 1817 (see St Buryan). The former BC chapel is on the other side of the triangle of roads through the hamlet from the Wesleyan chapel, and is now a farm building, having been also the Board School. The Morvah BC Circuit was later renamed Penzance.

MORWENSTOW

The eccentric poet-parson, Robert Stephen Hawker (1804-75), long enjoyed a love-hate relationship with his Methodist parishioners. When asked whether he would object to burying a Methodist, he replied, 'Not at all, I would like to bury all of them!' Yet his Methodist neighbours were among the first to come to his rescue when his vicarage caught fire. Hawker was a grandson of Dr Hawker of Plymouth, vicar of Charles Church, with whom John Wesley took tea in 1787.

In the churchyard there are memorials to early Bible Christian families, Corys of Holoborough, Cottles of Youlstone and others, as well as to church families such as the Canns. Their different theologies are well expressed by the Andrew Cory epitaph on the one hand and those of the two Richard Canns (surely composed by Parson Hawker) on the other. Andrew Cory was a Bible Christian travelling preacher who was drowned in the St Germans' river in 1833 at the age of 39. His epitaph reads: 'Early in life he was converted to God, was an acceptable and useful minister among the Bible Christians, and through the divine blessing on his labours many souls were truly converted to God, and so became the seals of his ministry ... Long as this stone shall bear his honoured name, or blade of grass upon this hillock grow, so long the passer-by shall speak his fame (and departing) say, A good man lies below.' Hawker came to the parish in the following year and could not have looked with favour on that inscription. His riposte, surely, is found on Richard Cann's tombstone (1838) which reads: '… Having been born of God by baptism of water and of the Holy Ghost, and by the ministry of an ordained clergyman of Christ, he kept his covenant like a Christian man. In the midst of much heresy and schism he did not depart from the faith once delivered …' The epitaph of the other Richard Cann (1842) is pure Hawker: 'Richard Cann of Lower Cory in this parish, yeoman, whose soul was carried by angels to Paradise … the second life which he received at the font he cherished in the chancel in as much that with certainty of the one true faith through the assurance of the blessed sacraments and in the safety of the ancient and apostolic worship of Christ in this consecrated sanctuary of God he clave steadfastly unto the Lord until "He was not for God took him." Sing from the chamber to the grave, Thus did the dead man say.' Johanna Brooks Neal (1787-1858) was converted through reading *Drelincourt on Death*, and soon afterwards stood up in her pew at church and gave an unexpected word of exhortation which resulted in her ejection by her husband and one of the church officers. She welcomed William O'Bryan to her home at Eastcott; she had been reading Ephesians 6.21 in her Bible, and she saw him as the Tychicus whom she expected God would send to her. Her gravestone is in the churchyard and tablets to her memory were formerly to be seen at Eastcott Chapel, now a private house. The one on the outside wall, which may still be there, read, 'In Memoriam Joanna Brooks Neal'. The other, now at Woodford Chapel, was erected by her family in thanksgiving for 'her consistent, devoted, and godly life and testimony in Morwenstow Church. She was one of the first members of the Bible Christian Connexion, with whom she continued for 43 years – from 1815 to 1858 – when she fell asleep in Jesus'.

MOUSEHOLE

A fishing village with a strong Methodist tradition. It was the home of William Carvosso (see Ponsanooth). At the annual Rogation Service St Clement's Methodist Church is decorated with ships' flags, and the pulpit made to resemble the bow of a ship. A fine set of stained glass windows include full-length figures of John Wesley and (perhaps unique in a Methodist church) John Wycliffe and John Bunyan. Another three Johns are commemorated by a brass tablet, unveiled in 1946: 'Keep in proud remembrance John Badcock, John Bryant, John Pearce, courageous young Methodists of Mousehole, who with Captain Allen F. Gardiner, R.N., in 1850 as servants of God sailed to Tierra Del Fuego, and there, sorely tried, with Christ-like fortitude proved themselves faithful unto death. Romans 8 vv 35-39.' Underneath the balcony on the front right-hand side there is a cross, a lectern and an eight-sided table on the panels of which are the names of the eight members of the crew of the *Solomon Browne* lifeboat who lost their lives in the Penlee disaster, 19 December 1981.

Jacob George, a class leader here in the nineteenth century, has a place in the history of the Cornish language as the writer of a manuscript, now at the British Library, entitled, 'Memoranda of Old Cornish words still current in Mousehole and Newlyn, 1868'. A rocky outcrop on the cliff appears on an old postcard entitled 'Wesley's Pulpit Rock' but for what reason we do not know. (See also Bristol.)

The art gallery and studio at Mount Zion is the former UMFC chapel which was opened in 1844 as a Teetotal Wesleyan chapel (see St Ives) and closed in 1987.

MULLION

Angrouse

Angrouse, a seventeenth-century farmhouse, on the road to Poldhu Cove, was the home of Wesley's hosts, Thomas and Ursula Triggs. Methodism had already reached Mullion when Ursula heard Wesley preach in Helston and invited him to her home. He came to Angrouse on 7 September 1762. Just inside the gateway of the field opposite the house is a stone marked 'S. T. 1762' which is held to mark the place where

Wesley preached – probably at 5 a.m. the following day. A Wesley Service is held in the field on the Sunday nearest to 7 September each year.

The present Methodist church was built by the United Methodist Free Churches in 1878. The dominant feature of its attractive interior, with the pews arranged in amphitheatre style, is a window depicting *Christ the Light of the World* (after Holman Hunt) in memory of Samuel Richard Matthews (1864-1942). An earlier window, 'In loving memory of those who loved and laboured faithfully for this Church', was dedicated in 1904 by the Revd Edward Boaden (see Cury). In the vestry is a wall tablet to the memory of John Thomas of Predannack (1815-86) and his wife Elizabeth who 'taught their children that to fear God was better than earthly possessions, and their sons that integrity of life was more acceptable than many prayers …'. A framed photograph in the vestry shows a group of five Sunday school teachers who, between them, had served the church for 280 years.

Mullion's first, and last, lifeboat and its house was the gift of Wesleyan Methodists in 1867 in response to an appeal which had been launched by the *Methodist Recorder* newspaper. The boat was named the Daniel J. Draper in memory of a Wesleyan minister who had been drowned in the Bay of Biscay in 1866. The Wesleyan chapel was on the east side of the village and is now flats.

MYLOR

Robert Terril Rundle (1811-96), Wesleyan

missionary to the Cree Indians in the Canadian Rockies, was born at Dowstall (see Across the Tamar p. 72). He was the grandson of William Carvosso (see Ponsanooth).

ST NEOT

The former Wesleyan chapel, some 120 yards to the east of the parish church, was built in 1814 and closed for adult worship in 1946, continuing until 1961 as the Sunday school. It is a neat slate-hung building and is now the pottery and craft shop of Mr and Mrs J. Greenwood. Methodist worship now takes place at a new chapel west of the bridge, built alongside the former Bible Christian chapel, which has become the Sunday school.

NEW MILL SW459344, Gulval

This former Methodist New Connexion wayside chapel, now a house, was built by the Teetotal Methodists (see St Ives) as its date stone still proclaims.

NEWLYN EAST

Richard Polwhele, the literary opponent of Methodism, was vicar here from 1821-38. A Methodist preaching pit, a small replica of Gwennap Pit, is on the south side of the road to Cubert, just beyond the cemetery. It was opened in 1852 as a memorial to the 36 men who lost their lives in the East Wheal Rose lead mine disaster in 1846.

The 1883 Wesleyan chapel closed in 1990, and the society reverted to the Sunday school building, which is itself the older chapel of 1832.

NEWLYN (Penzance)

The Wesleyan chapel (1832) had the 'London City Road' arrangement until 1950. The original pulpit is incorporated in the present rostrum. In the chapel is a tablet commemorating Mark Guy Pearse (1842-1930) who preached his last sermon there in 1926. 'Mark Guy' as he was widely known in Cornwall, was the Superintendent of the West London Mission, a popular preacher and lecturer, and a prolific writer of Cornish stories. He was the first Methodist minister to be made a bard of the Cornish Gorsedd; his bardic name, 'Pyscajor a Dus', means Fisher of Men. He was born in Camborne where his father of the same name was a chemist. His forefathers were Pearses of Camelford.

The chapel became unsafe in the 1990s, and worship was relocated to the schoolroom. A major renovation and community premises scheme is in hand.

Centenary Chapel is the former Primitive Methodist chapel, built in 1928 to replace Ebenezer Chapel in Boase Street, which had been opened in 1835. For many years Ebenezer continued to be used as the Sunday school but it was finally sold in the late 1980s, and is used as a fishing company's store.

NEWQUAY

Methodism in Newquay began in a fisherman's cottage close to the harbour but came to nothing. It was reintroduced by the freelance evangelist William O'Bryan in his Wesleyan days. The first chapel was built in 1833 and is now a Salvation

Army barracks in Crantock Street. It once had a bell-turret like the one at Port Isaac.

The present Newquay Wesley Church (by Bell, Withers and Meredith of London) was opened in East Street in 1904 on what was to become a central site in the rapidly growing holiday resort. The building has a tower, but the intended spire and belfry did not materialize. It consists of nave, chancel, sanctuary and transepts. The font (1939) is of Cornish stone, slate, serpentine and granite, and is in memory of Henry Chegwidden. There is a series of stained glass windows, several of them the gift of the Revd and Mrs W. Hodson Smith in memory of Mr Smith's parents and theological tutors, and of the Revd Charles Garrett of the Liverpool Mission. The sanctuary window is a representation of Holman Hunt's *Christ the Light of the World*. Rays of light are seen radiating from Christ on to the figures of the four evangelists and the angel of the nativity. In the west aisle is the window of the Virgin and Child (1973) given in memory of Marjorie and Alfred Chegwin. The five windows in the gallery relate to the parable of the Good Samaritan. A note of unintended humour is raised by the second and third inscriptions which read in sequence, 'He passed by on the other side' and 'Go and do thou likewise'.

The organ was first built by John Snetzler for Andover Parish Church in 1772. Its subsequent rebuildings are listed on a tablet fixed to the organ case: 'John Snetzler, 1772; Bevingtons of London, 1882; Hele and Co., Plymouth,

1904; Griffin and Stroud, 1937; Lance Foy of Truro, 1979'.

NORTH TAMERTON
Wesley preached in the parish church in 1745 and 1747 and then, in 1750, 'because the church key was a mile off' and the rector was absent, he preached in 'a large room' adjoining the church. This room is now a barn.

PADSTOW
A port of embarkation for emigrants from north Cornwall including a number of Bible Christian missionaries. One such company sailed for Quebec in 1846, shortly before May Day when the ancient ceremony of the 'Obby 'Oss is performed. They congratulated themselves that they had avoided the old pagan ceremony, but some of the crew were Padstow men and they produced their own 'Obby 'Oss on the deck on 1 May. The Bible Christian miller, Thomas Tregaskis, tried unsuccessfully to bribe the Padstow people to give up their ancient custom in 1845 in return for an annual gift of a bullock to provide roast beef.

The Bible Christian chapel in Ruthy's Lane closed about 1934 when the society united with the former Wesleyan society. The building is now a Masonic Lodge. The Wesleyan chapel became unsafe in 1987, and was demolished for a car park. The former schoolroom became the chapel.

PAUL
Kerris Roundago SW445/273 is an Iron Age round in which Wesley is said to have preached. To reach the site, take the

B3315 from Newlyn for a mile and turn right at the Kerris signpost. Continue for a further mile to the Roundago, close to the former Kerris Wesleyan chapel.

In the village of Sheffield there was a Teetotal Wesleyan chapel (see St Ives), which became part of the Methodist New Connexion. It closed in 1955.

PELYNT

The gravestone of Philip Hawke (1749-1827), in the churchyard near the tower, described him as 'The first person in the parish who opened his house to the Wesleyan Methodist preachers who after passing several years in obloquy and persecution for righteousness' sake, outlived the tongue of slander, saw a society formed, chapel erected and sinners converted, then died in peace beloved and lamented'. The inscription is now hard to read but it is hoped that a plaque might be erected nearby recording the inscription.

PENCOYS SW688384

In the parish church is the organ formerly at Chili Road UMFC Church, Illogan Highway, on which the composer Thomas Merritt must have played his Christmas carols (see Illogan).

PENPONDS SW637392

Wesley is said to have stayed with Richard Trevithick (1735-97), a mine manager and Methodist class leader, whose (thatched) house at Penponds is marked by a plaque as the birthplace of his son of the same name, the inventor of the high pressure boiler and the steam locomotive.

PENRYN

Wesley came to Penryn by boat in 1745 (see Falmouth) and on later visits preached, it is thought, near the present square. According to tradition he stayed with Mrs Rapson in Tresooth Lane. A town map dated 1690 shows a bowling green with trees on two sides at the bottom of Quay Hill which answers well to Wesley's description of his preaching place in 1757, (standing before Mr H's door) 'an extremely pleasant place on the side of a hill, commanding a fruitful vale, the opposite hills, and Falmouth Harbour. Tall trees hung over me, and surrounded a bowling green which was behind me.' A church Methodist lady called Mrs Busvine, who attended St Gluvias Church, displeased the vicar by quoting John Wesley against him!

PENZANCE

Until 1871 the town was part of Madron parish. Wesley's preaching sites in Penzance cannot all be identified; 'in a meadow', 'on a cliff', 'at the end of the town' are all inexact descriptions. 'The gentleman's balcony' which 'commanded the market place' was probably at the Star Inn in Market Jew Street. The balcony was removed in 1860. He also preached on the Western Green, fronting the coast towards Newlyn, in 1747, and was in imminent danger from the mob, but was rescued by Philip Kelynack, a Newlyn man, known locally as 'Old Bunger', and young Peter Jaco, also from Newlyn, who became one of his preachers (see London). At the top of Market Jew Street is a statue of Sir Humphry Davy (1778-1829), the inventor of the miners' safety lamp and President of the Royal Society. According to family tradition Humphry, as a child, received John Wesley's blessing after church service.

Chapel Street Methodist Church was built by the Wesleyans in 1814 and largely rebuilt in 1864. The street takes its name from the Anglican St Mary's chapel, now the parish church, but once a chapel in Madron parish. The interior of the Methodist chapel, probably from the beginning, was arranged in the 'London City Road' style with the pulpit in front of the Communion table. It retained its central double-decker pulpit until 1964 when the pulpit and reading desk were separated and moved to either side to open up a view of the sanctuary. The eight windows along the sides of the church, and presumably the corresponding ones in the gallery above, were filled with coloured glass by H.J. Salisbury, of London and St Albans, in 1914, and these, together with the earlier window in the sanctuary, depict scenes from the life of Christ whilst those in the gallery show saints of the Old and New Testaments. The two-light window above the Communion table depicts Christ as King and as the Good Shepherd. On either side of this central window are tablets of the Ten Commandments on the one side (in place of the Commandments of Jesus in City Road chapel) and the Lord's Prayer and Apostles' Creed on the other. This galaxy of colour, depicting the life of Christ on earth and the whole company of the saints in heaven, will remind some travellers of an Eastern Orthodox more than a Cornish Methodist interior.

There are several memorial tablets of interest. Two of them, mounted on a single slab, commemorate William Carne (1754-1836) and his son Joseph Carne FRS (1789-1865). William was a wealthy banker who heeded Wesley's advice to gain, save and give, for it is estimated that he gave away over £10,000. He entertained Wesley on his last visit to Cornwall and served as circuit steward in years as far apart as 1785 and 1834. For many years he was a leading layman in the Cornwall District and was said to have borne 'a paternal relationship' to Cornish Methodism.

At either side of the sanctuary are marble memorials to two young Wesleyan ministers. The one on the left commemorates Richard Treffry, Junior, (1804-38), a young minister of great promise who was forced to retire early through ill-health and came to live at No. 3 Clarence Terrace. He died in 1838 at the age of 34 and was buried in St Mary's churchyard alongside his infant daughter. The gravestone is now laid flat by the pathway near the rear entrance: it has what is perhaps the most touching epitaph in a Cornish churchyard – simply the scriptural text, 2 Kings 4.26 – 'Is it well with thy husband? Is it well with the child? And she answered, It is well.' Richard was a son of Richard Treffry of Tregony, the President of the Conference in 1833. He wrote several biographies which contain useful information about Cornish Methodism. One of his closely written manuscripts, on 'Ministerial Power in the Excision of Unworthy Members of the Church' is now at the

RIC, Truro. His memorial at Chapel Street reads, 'Sacred to the memory of the Rev Richard Treffry, Jun. … born at Camelford 1804 … died at Penzance 1838 … As a Christian he was richly adorned with the graces of the Holy Spirit … as a Christian Minister he was clear, comprehensive, eloquent and faithful … As a Christian Author he discovered a compass of knowledge, an accuracy and patience of research and a steadfast adherence to the pure truth of revelation which entitle him to an honourable rank among the ablest advocates of the faith …'.

To the right of the sanctuary is a memorial to a young missionary who died in West Africa, as so many did at a time when the Gold Coast was known as 'the white man's grave'. Samuel Symons was a local preacher at Penzance before entering the ministry and going to West Africa. He served for two years on McCarthy's Island in the River Gambia and died there in 1844 aged 29.

The commemorative windows in the body of the church were donated by individuals and groups. The Nicodemus window was presented by the Wesley Guild and the 'Holman Hunt' window was given 'in memory of the Mistresses and Girls of West Cornwall College who worshipped in this church from 1884-1914'. A blazer badge of the school is framed and fixed to the adjoining wall. A further brass plate records that the Children's Chapel has been furnished to commemorate West Cornwall School, 1884-1967.

Adjoining the Resurrection window are two brass tablets which come as a surprise to many people. One of them reads: 'To commemorate the Bi-Centenary of the birth of Maria Branwell, born Penzance 1783, died Haworth 1821, a member of the Penzance Wesleyan Society and mother of the Brontës'. The other tablet is 'In memory of Elizabeth Branwell, born Penzance 1776, died Haworth 1842. A member of the Penzance Wesleyan Society, elder sister of Maria. From 1821 until her death she dedicated herself to the upbringing and welfare of the motherless Brontë children. This plaque is the gift of The Brontë Society, Haworth, Yorkshire.' The Resurrection window itself was given in memory of Mary Branwell of Redinnick House by her brothers, Frederick and Robert, and to complete the Branwell series is a brass tablet (to the left of the window) to Hugh Branwell (1890-1966), 'the organist of this Church for 42 years' presented by his sister, Frances Cathrina Branwell.

25 Chapel Street was the home of Thomas Branwell, some of whose Methodist Magazines were no doubt among those taken to Haworth parsonage to be included in the early reading of the Brontë sisters –'those mad Methodist magazines' as they considered them. Another of Branwell's daughters was the wife of John Fennell, a class leader at Chapel Street and later a schoolmaster at the Wesleyan Woodhouse Grove School, Yorkshire.

Richmond Wesleyan Church was built in Tolver Place about 150 yards from

High Street (see below) in 1907 in the 'arts and crafts' Gothic style – architects Gunton and Gordon, London. Altar curtains were numbered among its furnishings. When it opened the Wesleyans had within ? mile of each other the City Road style Chapel Street building, 'arts and crafts' style Richmond and a Salvation Army style mission room in New Street, parallel to Chapel Street to the north, opened at the end of the nineteenth century and closed in 1937. This building is now a small warehouse. West of Chapel Street is Queen Street where the Wesleyan chapel in use before Chapel Street is now the Salvation Army Citadel. After the Wesleyan Methodist Association split in 1835, its congregation used the Queen Street premises before moving to the Parade Street site (see below).

High Street Church, (architect, John W. Trounson) was built by the Bible Christians in 1879, and was their Conference chapel in 1890 and 1900. The UMFC church in Parade Street (architect, Oliver Caldwell) was rebuilt in 1889 to its present frontage, but closed in 1967 to become a theatre and arts centre. Alexandra Road Church (1903, architect, James Firth, Oldham) was the last Methodist New Connexion chapel to be built in Cornwall. It closed in 1995 and is now flats. The former Primitive Methodist chapel in Mount Street was built in 1839, extended several times, and finally closed in 1968; it is now a second-hand furniture shop and flats.

Wesley Rock Chapel is at Heamoor, a mile from Penzance on the Madron road. The pulpit stands on a block of granite on which a tablet is fixed inscribed, 'On this rock Mr Wesley and others preached the Gospel of Christ, A. D. 1743-1760. Luke 14C 23v. W. Pengelly, 1840'. The stone was originally in a nearby field and was moved into the first Hea Moor Chapel (now the schoolroom) when it was built in 1842. It was moved again, in 1896, into the present chapel. The dates given in the inscription may be questioned but Wesley did preach at Hea in April 1744. In the chapel yard is a memorial to the Revd James Akerman whose son, Sir James Akerman, was a founder of the colony of Natal.

The former Bible Christian chapel on the corner of Joseph's Lane and Chapel Road, Heamoor, was opened in 1863, following an earlier chapel in Polmennor Road which may have been built by the Boylites (see St Buryan). All that remains of the earlier chapel is four low walls defining a car pound. The second chapel closed in 1960, when the society amalgamated with the Wesleyans 100 yards away, and the building is now a private house.

West Cornwall School for Girls was opened in Chapel Street in 1884 and moved to the York House estate c.1931. It was closed in 1967; the buildings are now the Municipal Offices.

PERRANWELL SW774392,
Perranarworthal
Wesley preached to 'a very large congregation' here, probably on the village green, in 1747.

The large Wesley chapel (Architect James Hicks of Redruth; compare Porthleven) was sold in 1998, when the building became too much for the small society. The property became a nursery school, but the society still worships in it on Sunday. The former Bible Christian society at Chyvogue joined with Wesley in 1968. The chapel was sold, and flats now stand on the site.

PERRANZABULOE SW765534

The large Wesleyan chapel standing on the hillside at Bolingey is now a block of flats. Some of the families who worshipped there in the 1850s are described in W.D. Tyack's *The Miner of Perranzabuloe*. One of the leaders was William Murrish, whose gravestone in Perran churchyard links him immediately with the book: 'Here rest the mortal remains of William Murrish 'The Miner of Perran-Zabuloe' who died on the 6th of May 1861 aged 43 years. He lived a Christian and his end was peace'.

A marble tablet in the parish church lists the names of the chief benefactors to the church when it was rebuilt at Lambourne in 1805, and among them is William Cowlin of Callestick who gave £31 10s. He was the father-in-law of William O'Bryan, the Bible Christian founder. The last wedding to be held in the old church in the sands on 3 July 1803 was that of William O'Bryan and Catherine Cowlin. During the service a heifer walked in and joined them at the altar. The scant remains of the church (not to be confused with the buried oratory close by) can still be seen.

PHILLACK

Joseph Grieves, who introduced Primitive Methodism to St Ives in 1829, spent three hours in prayer in Phillack Church (in the sandhills) and then a strong man – surely a St Christopher! – offered to carry him across the river. Notice the copper slag blocks in the churchyard wall and nearby buildings. Wesley thought that the Hayle preaching house, built with this material 'would last as long as the earth'.

The 'Boylites' (see St Buryan) probably had a chapel at High Lanes, then in the parish, on the south-east side of Hayle; there was most certainly a Bible Christian chapel there later (see Hayle).

POLPERRO

Wesley visited Polperro twice: in 1762 when he is thought to have preached from the balcony of the house of Samuel Coad, a blacksmith, in Little Green, and in 1768 when he visited the house of John Rommet, a fisherman and fish curer. Rommet's house, now called 'The Anchorage', is in the Warren and can be identified from the harbourside by its bow front. Wesley declined Rommet's invitation to stay overnight because 'the aroma was too pungent for me'. Instead he stayed at a house on Talland Hill. There is a tradition that he also preached at Ways End.

Polperro's best known resident was Dr Jonathan Couch (1789-1870), the local doctor, naturalist, zoologist, ichthyologist, botanist, archaeologist, classical scholar and grandfather of 'Q' (Sir Arthur Quiller Couch) of Cambridge.

Dr Couch was born in the house now called Warren Cottage, and later lived in the Green. A Methodist, Dr Couch identified himself with the Wesleyan reformers of 1835 and became the natural leader of the Wesleyan Methodist Association when it arrived at Polperro in 1837. The seceders held their meetings in a room above the Old Market House in the Green, which they called 'The Refuge', the building which has now unfortunately attracted to itself, quite mistakenly, the name of John Wesley. In 1838 they opened the chapel at the foot of Talland Hill, now occupied by the Iben Estate Agency. Note the date stone over the door. Curiously, this Association chapel was opened by William O'Bryan, the Bible Christian leader, on one of his many return trips to Cornwall after emigrating to the USA in 1831.

Ebenezer Bible Christian Chapel (1877-1934) is now the Ebenezer Gallery of the East Cornwall Society of Artists. It is on the west side of the road going down from the car park.

POLZEATH
War memorials are frequently found in Methodist chapels but at Polzeath an oak plaque recalls a different aspect of the last war; it reads: '1940. Presented by East Ham County Borough Council to commemorate the kindness shown to the children of Aldersbrook Homes by the residents of Polzeath during the war years, 1940-46'.

PONSANOOTH
A glass case in the chapel contains a copy of a book which had a great influence on Cornish Methodists a century ago: *The Efficacy of Faith in the Atonement of Christ exemplified in a Memoir of Mr William Carvosso* (1835).

William Carvosso (1750-1834) was born at Mousehole and came to St Gluvias in 1788 to farm Cosawes Barton. He arranged for Methodist services to be held at his house and took the lead in building a chapel at Ponsanooth in 1813. He and his wife are buried in the chapel yard, close to the wall of the present church which was built in 1843. In his retirement he taught himself to write and soon became a diarist and a prolific letter writer. A class leader at Ponsanooth but not a preacher, he travelled widely through the county and was accepted by many as a spiritual counsellor.

PORT ISAAC
Wesley paid many visits to Port Isaac where he stayed with Richard Wood (died 1807), a local merchant who had a house and yard in the town, and was probably engaged in trade between Bristol and the china clay area (see Bristol). It is not possible to identify this property with any certainty. It may have been in the courtyard on the left side of Middle Street, going up towards the Dolphin, but Victoria House, on the elbow of Fore Street, facing up the hill, has also long been associated with Wesley, and it is said that he preached there from a balcony. It would be reasonable to assume that he also preached on the Platt from the stone steps beside the old fish cellars, as open-air speakers in Port Isaac have always done.

Roscarrock Hill Chapel with its bell turret was built by the Wesleyan Methodist Association reformers in 1837. It caught the eye of John Betjeman who wrote: 'A simple slate Methodist chapel and Sunday School in the Georgian tradition, hangs over the harbour and is the prettiest building in the town.' Above the double flight of steps leading to the old chapel (latterly the schoolroom) is the belfry containing the bell salvaged from the wreck of the Bencoolen merchantman off Bude in 1862.

Roscarrock Hill Chapel showing belfry

The church closed in 1992 and is now a pottery; the schoolroom is a private house. The bell, and its story told on a framed illuminated scroll can be seen in the pottery. The former Wesley chapel has also been converted to a house with part of its schoolroom walls surrounding an attractive landscaped garden. Its bell, marked 'W & H 1800.B' (? Bristol), which formerly hung in the turret, is now in the CMHA Museum at Carharrack (q.v.).

PORTHLEVEN

An iron-work house sign at the corner of Looe Bar Road and Mounts Road, facing the bay – The Old Chapel, 1790-1820 – draws attention to what was the

first Methodist chapel at Porthleven. The later chapel (1840) in The Gue became the schoolroom of Fore Street Wesleyan Church when it opened in 1883. It was sold in 1999, and is being converted to residential use.

The Bible Christians had their chapel in Peverell Road from 1863. An earlier building was in use by 1828 at a site not now identifiable, but may have been lost to the Arminian Bible Christians (see Breage). Peverell Road closed in 1989, and the building is being converted to residential use.

Features of Methodist life in Porthleven have included the Methodist celebration of St Peterstide on the weekend following the saint's day, an event once seeing some competition between the two chapels, but having in recent years become an ecumenical event, and the celebration of the Harvest of the Sea on the last Sunday in October. The chapel is decorated in a maritime theme, featuring an imitation bow of a boat and a wheelhouse erected around the pulpit, both pieces of woodwork coming from Peverell Road.

PORTHTOWAN

The society at Porthtowan was founded by Thomas Garland (1771-1827), a mine captain and class leader whose memorial can be seen at Bridge, Illogan. A delightful account of its early days can be found in *Foolish Dick, the Pilgrim Preacher*, by S.W. Christophers, published in 1873. Garland started the class after 'Aunt' Betty Chegwin told him that 't'wud be the salvaashun of my sawl' if he would do that. Thomas Chegwin, a member of her family, was one of the founders of Methodism in Portugal.

The chapel, built in 1820, is the lower building on the left. It will always be associated with Richard Hampton (1782-1858), better known as 'Foolish Dick' whose undoubted simplicity was accompanied by shafts of native wit. Two young men once seated themselves on either side of him on a form and one said, 'We don't know whether you are a knave or a fool.' Quickly he replied, 'Right at this moment I am between the two!' Foolish Dick had a small part in building the chapel, until he ran the wheelbarrow over his foot! Despite his disabilities, 'the poor idjut', as he called himself, though not a local preacher, was accepted on the plan by special dispensation. He travelled through Cornwall on preaching tours and was generally acceptable. The present chapel complex at Porthtowan is rather unusual; the two linked buildings are not a chapel and a former chapel now a schoolroom, as is so often the case, but two chapels which can only be described as the winter chapel (that of 1820) and the summer chapel built in 1980.

On the bicentenary of the society in 1996 the former President, the Revd Amos Cresswell, planted a memorial cherry tree at the corner of the car park.

POUNDSTOCK
Penfound is a medieval house in which both Wesley and Whitefield are said to have preached. A plaster cast of George Whitefield was placed over the inner door of the porch by Nicholas Penfound of Penfound.

QUENCHWELL
This former Bible Christian chapel was opened in 1906, when the 1907 union of the Bible Christians, the Methodist New Connexion and the United Methodist Free Churches was imminent – and the carved inscription, BIBLE CHRISTIAN MEMORIAL CHAPEL, should be read in this light. It closed in 1999, and is being used by the Cornish Russian Orthodox Congregation.

REDRUTH
Wesley's usual preaching place in the town was at the entrance to the market house in Fore Street, approximately in the position of the clock tower. He also preached from the balcony at Bank House, West End. He was at St Euny Church in 1750 where he heard the rector preach 'an exceedingly useful sermon on the General Judgement'. He heard another 'excellent sermon' there in 1755, and was present in 1757 when there were a number of French prisoners in the congregation. Between these last two dates the church, though not the tower, had been completely rebuilt and assumed its present Georgian appearance. Charles Wesley attended evening service at St Euny in 1746. In the church is a copy of a portrait of John Collins, the rector from 1734 to 1775, who had known Wesley at Oxford. On the outside east wall of the church is the gravestone of Andrew and Elizabeth Harper who lived in Fore Street and were among Wesley's hosts in Redruth. Wesley published 'Extracts' from Elizabeth Harper's Journal which

he thought illustrated the meaning of Christian Perfection. Across the path nearby is the tombstone of Francis Woolf who for a time was one of Wesley's travelling preachers, but who afterwards returned to Redruth and became a peruke maker in Fore Street (see Bristol p. 72).

Wesley visited Trewirgie House, the home of the Jenkin family who later became Quakers, and baptized one of their children. On one occasion he hired a chaise from the London Inn and set out on a journey to St Ives which almost ended in disaster at the Hayle estuary (see Hayle). Wesley Chapel (1826) has a medallion Wesley window in the upper schoolroom. In the chapel itself is an urn-shaped memorial to Thomas Garland (1804-65), the editor of the *Cornubian* newspaper from 1830-32. As at Camborne and Carharrack, the original 'City Road' arrangement of the sanctuary with the Ten Commandments on the wall behind the Communion table was disturbed by the introduction of a Victorian rostrum. In the schoolroom is a finely carved slate decalogue table, signed 'Amos Nicholls, Penryn Street, 1827' from the old Primitive Methodist Chapel (now called Chapel House at Plain-an-Gwary). Jim's Cash and Carry Store in Fore Street was the Wesleyan Association Chapel from 1839 to 1865. It was succeeded in 1865 by a larger and prestigious Grecian style chapel on the opposite side of Fore Street in which the United Methodist Free Churches Conference met in 1889 and 1901, and the United Methodist Conference in 1914 and 1931. Samuel

Sebastian Wesley opened its organ in 1873. No trace of this building now remains on what is now the Fore Street car park, but the decorative flowerpots which surmounted the 'Flower Pot Chapel' are in Victoria Park. The former Bible Christian chapel on Treruffe Hill closed in 1975 and is being converted into flats.

In the Cornwall Centre in Alma Street is the Cornwall Studies Library, where the important collection of books deposited on permanent loan by the Cornish Methodist Historical Association is held.

RILLA MILL
The interior of the Wesleyan chapel (1846 and 1866) was rearranged in 1952 when the sanctuary was panelled with former pew doors and an amber cross was placed in the window above. A wall tablet recalls that the Revd Dr F. Luke Wiseman, the second President of the Methodist Conference (and some would say one of the last of the great preachers of Wesleyan Methodism) preached his first sermon here as a youth of 17. Stanley Sowton (1875-1958) the Assistant Financial Secretary at the Mission House, well known to the children of Methodism as 'Uncle Ned', lived at Westcott during his retirement. A man of ideas and unbounding energy who had a 'hot line' to influential people in Methodism at the time, he was the inspiration behind the restoration and reopening of the Isbell Cottage at Altarnun (see Trewint).

RINSEY SW595273
This hamlet on Mount's Bay was at one time the home of a community of

Methodist smugglers and their families, the Carters and Richards prominent among them. Prussia Cove nearby was the base of their operations. Brandy and rum were brought from Roscoff on the French coast. Captain Harry Carter's adventurous story is told in *The Autobiography of a Cornish Smuggler*. His watch and teapot are in the County Museum, Truro. (See also Fowey and Trevean.) The ex-UMFC chapel here closed in 1950, and the building is now holiday accommodation.

ROCHE

Samuel Furly, the rector here from 1766-95, and his sister Dorothy were among Wesley's correspondents. He spent an evening with them at the rectory in 1768. Furly's tombstone is in the churchyard near the boundary hedge opposite the south porch. Like Furly, his successor Richard Postlethwaite (1800-19) had excellent relations with the Methodists.

ROSEMERGY SW 418364

John and Alice Daniel's house

The home of John and Alice Daniel who entertained John Wesley and added two rooms to their house for the use of Wesley and the preachers, is on the coastal side of the road from St Ives to St Just. According to tradition when Wesley first came past the house, in 1744, he found Alice Daniel collecting honey and stopped to speak to her about 'things sweeter than honey or the honeycomb'.

He visited Rosemergy again in later years when Alice was old and blind and preached near the house. It was at Rosemergy that William Crabb, one of the preachers, who was being pursued by the constable of St Just, hastily changed horses and so eluded his pursuer. The house has recently been restored in eighteenth-century style. It is not open to the public except by special arrangement. The bedroom Wesley used, together with its furnishings, was long left unaltered. A table from the room is now at the Isbell cottage (see Trewint), and a slate (a Cornish 'hellan') taken from over Wesley's bedroom is in the Museum of Cornish Methodism at Carharrack.

ROSEWORTHY SW616397

The once much admired and photographed thatched chapel on the road from Camborne to Hayle was closed in 1975 and the property allowed to fall into a ruinous state. It is now a house and, happily, has been so expertly and carefully restored to its original appearance that it still attracts the attention of passers-by.

RUTHERNBRIDGE

The birthplace of Walter Lawry (1793-1859), pioneer Wesleyan missionary in New Zealand and the Friendly Islands (see also Gorran). The young Adam

Clarke had a serious fall from his horse, which had previously belonged to John Wesley, on Ruthern Downs. He road on in great discomfort to Port Isaac where Dr Twentyman bled him and discussed alchemy with him.

RUTHVOES SW925605
The former Bible Christian chapel in this hamlet closed in 2001 and is being converted into a house. It is, though, one of a decreasing number of chapels still to carry a 'BC' date plaque in the form of an open book (a Bible?) with the hard-to-read inscription 'BC1901'.

SALTASH
Wesley stayed at Saltash one stormy night in 1760 because 'no boat would venture out', and the following morning, there being no improvement, he rode on to New Bridge, at Gunnislake. In 1775 Methodists from Plymouth Dock (Devonport) sent a boat to collect him at Saltash.

Saltash Methodist Church, 1990

After the Second World War the Methodist church was rebuilt with money from the National War Damage Fund and the Wesley Hall was added in 1958. One of its windows was made from parts of a larger stained glass window (1869-70) from the war-damaged church of St James the Great at Devonport. In 1989 the whole of the premises were demolished and a new church complex with ancillary buildings, including a sports hall, was opened in January 1990 (architect, Francis Bush of Plymouth).

A carpeted foyer leads into the church. The St James window is still a feature in the new church, and another is a three-manual pipe organ, with over 2,000 pipes, built by Maurice Egglington. A tall steel cross rises from the apex of the building. At the south end of St Stephen's churchyard is a stone inscribed: 'Here are laid to rest the remains of persons formerly buried in the old Wesleyan Methodist Cemetery, Waterloo Road, Saltash, when that land was incorporated in the building of the Tamar Bridge, September 1959'.

SENNEN
After three weeks of misty weather Charles Wesley went early to bed at Sennen, and wrote on the following morning, 'I saw a strange sight, the sun shining in Cornwall.'

SHEVIOCK
A deeply recessed window in the parish church contains a portrait of John Wesley, placed there in memory of Florence Gertrude Hart (1897-1960).

SITHNEY
Two vicars of Sithney had Methodist associations: William Newton, who hired a mob to attack the Methodists in 1746, and John Pearce (1913-85) who, himself being of Methodist descent, was a great admirer of the Wesleys and the editor of their Cornish journeys – see *The Wesleys in Cornwall* (1964). He

was the first Chairman of the Cornish Methodist Historical Association. Wesley preached in the parish several times, on one occasion, according to tradition, standing on a stone slab now in the grounds at Trevarno.

The Wesleyan chapel on the west side of the road leading south out of the village ceased to be used in 1974, and after using the schoolroom for several years the society amalgamated with Troon, Breage, in 1991 and the combined society adopted the hybrid name 'Breaney'.

ST STEPHEN'S COOMBE SW950513

In 1757 Wesley recorded that he had preached 'at St Stephen's near a lone house on the side of a barren mountain'. This is thought to have been at the foot of the steep hillside at Coombe which can best be seen on the left after passing under the railway arch on the road to Hewas Water. The railway embankment was made, of course, at a later date.

According to a family tradition Wesley had tea with the Yellands at the old house which used to stand on the left side of the road running north eastwards towards High Street, immediately before you come to Chapel House. This was the original Wesleyan chapel built in 1833, but in 1851, during the disruption that followed the 'Fly Sheet Controversy' this chapel passed to the Wesleyan Reformers. The date stone shows signs of alteration, for it now reads 'Coombe / UM… / 1833'. Presumably it had read at least UMFC prior to 1907. The chapel

closed in the 1930s. A little further towards High Street, on the opposite side of the road, is the private house called 'Old Sunday School Cottage'.

After losing the chapel the Wesleyans moved south west, to just past the turning for the railway arch, where in 1859 they opened a new chapel. Enlarged in 1880, it was abandoned about 1997, when the congregation moved across the road to the newer Sunday school building.

STITHIANS

John Wesley paid several visits to Stithians. In 1744 he preached from a wall surrounding a green triangular plot which is thought to have been on Penmennor farm at the back of Hendra chapel. A rock in the field there used to be pointed out as the place where he stood. The only triangular piece of land is now the graveyard. Charles Wesley was in Stithians in 1746. The two chapels, Hendra (Wesleyan; 1814), now converted to flats, and Penmennor (UMFC; 1865) stand in close proximity to each other some distance out of the village to the north west. Chapels which originated in the reform movements of 1834 and 1849 were often built close to the one from which the members had seceded or been expelled – as at Redruth and Delabole.

An unusual marble memorial consisting of a pillar surmounted by a 'drum' and on top of that a 'candlestick with a flame' was in Hendra Wesleyan Church until it closed in 1976, and is now in the parish church. It commemorates Albert Charles Collins (1856-1937), a member of the church who later became a successful businessman in Johannesburg. Collins and his partner, William Mountstephens, were public benefactors both in South Africa and in this country – St Stithians College, Johannesburg, is their foundation.

TEMPLE
The isolated hamlet of Temple lies on a short stretch of the old road on the top of Bodmin Moor, bypassed by the A30. The closed Bible Christian chapel ('Olde Chapel Farm') is typical of the rural nature of many of the chapels of that denomination. (See also Innis.)

THREEMILESTONE
This Methodist church near Truro (SW780450) is a dual-purpose building opened in 1974 and enlarged in 1984 – architect, K.E. Rundle of Truro.

TORPOINT
After renovations in 1999, this chapel reopened as the Cornerstone Church.

TOWEDNACK
Charles Wesley, in 1743, sat six feet from the pulpit and listened to Parson Hoblyn describing the Methodist preachers as false prophets. After the service Wesley addressed a group of people outside the church. He returned the following Sunday and was attacked by 'the minister's mob' wielding sticks and throwing stones. The former Wesleyan chapel closed in 1971; it is now a private house.

TOWNSHEND
The 1871 Wesleyan chapel closed in 1990, and has been converted into a private house. Two memorial plaques removed from the interior and re-erected to the right of the gate bear testimony to the Great Emigration of Cornish folk in the nineteenth and early twentieth centuries. One records the death in France in August 1918 of Josiah Mitchell (30), son of William H. and Marina of Townshend while Josiah was serving with 18 Battalion of the Canadian Regiment. The other records the death in Montana, USA, of Abraham Winn (36), accidentally killed working as a miner. No local relatives are mentioned.

Opposite the 1871 chapel is the original chapel of circa 1800, latterly the Sunday school, but now in use as the village hall.

TREBULLETT (Lezant)
John Husband (1751-1818), a yeoman farmer who had heard Wesley preach, built the first chapel here in 1806. On his gravestone it is recorded that 'as a man he possessed an intelligent mind. As a Christian he happily enjoyed those sound principles which reform'd his practice: he was liberal in his sentiments yet was a decided Methodist for 40 years (he devoted this plot of ground to be the repository for the dead in which he was by an unerring Providence the first interred) retaining his confidence in God and triumphing in hope of eternal felicity. He died of an imposthume December 28th 1818 aged 67 years'.

TREDRUSTON (St Breock)
The farmhouse, an early Methodist preaching place, was visited by William

O'Bryan and later became a centre of Bible Christian work.

TREEN (St Levan)

A small, plain but attractive Wesleyan chapel, built in 1834 by a brother and sister, William and Bathsheba Richards, out of legacies they had both received from 'a miser'.

TREGADILLETT SX297841

An Anglican-Methodist Local Ecumenical Project began here in 1986, and uses a new worship centre in the village which opened in 2004.

TREGEARE SX244867

This secluded and attractive Wesleyan chapel and burial ground closed in 1997. To the left of the path from the entrance is the grave of Thomas Adams of Lidcot (1788-1859) and his wife Tabitha. Like the Isbells at Trewint, the family were Church Methodists and Thomas was a class leader at Pipers Pool. They were the parents of John Couch Adams, the Cambridge astronomer and discoverer of the planet Neptune (see Laneast and Truro Cathedral), and Thomas Adams, an early Wesleyan missionary in Tonga. It is possible that John Wesley preached on the Green at Tregeare in 1747 (as a local tradition suggests) and in Tregeare House in 1755 (see Launceston).

TREGONY

Newton (SW947457) was the birthplace of Richard Treffry (1771-1842), the President of the Wesleyan Conference in 1833. His framed portrait with a few biographical details can be seen in the church porch. The former Wesleyan chapel opened in 1824. The Bible Christian chapel in the village was opened 12 years later, and closed in 1935 when the societies united.

Treffry's early diary, covering his Cornish and Welsh circuits from 1802-09 is still preserved. Tregony was one of the rotten boroughs; when he was there on 18 July 1802, Treffry found a society which had been strong 'but now, through the [recent] elections, many are grown weary and others totally dead'.

TRELIGGA SX051845

A simple stone and slate-walled chapel built in 1829, now a farm building, which has its date stone still in position over the doorway. In 1835 the local Wesleyan Association reformers obtained a legal injunction forbidding the Wesleyan superintendent access to the building and this they nailed to the chapel door. The document was for a long time framed as a curiosity on the wall of the Methodist Property Office in Manchester. The Bible Christians opened a new chapel here in 1902, but it closed in 1970. Abraham Bastard, a former champion wrestler, was a member at the older chapel and used his great strength to protect the first Bible Christians and their preachers from their assailants.

TRELILL

A typical Cornish chapel on the road from St Kew Highway to Delabole. Built in 1812, it was successively Wesleyan Methodist, Wesleyan Methodist Association, United Methodist Free Church, United Methodist and

Methodist. The chapel closed in 1990 and is now a private house. This Guide's original compiler was married here.

Trelill Chapel, 1812-1990

TRENEGLOS SX 191897
The first Bethel Bible Christian chapel, now the schoolroom, was opened by James Thorne in 1838. Prominent in the graveyard is a granite obelisk commemorating John and Catherine Worden, two of the leading members of the early society. The present chapel was opened in 1881.

TRESILLIAN
The Hunkin family Bible kept at the chapel marks the association of Joseph Weston Hunkin, a Truro local preacher (who had some of the characteristics of Billy Bray), and his son Joseph Wellington Hunkin (the eighth bishop of Truro), with Tresillian. Dr Hunkin, as a preacher on trial, conducted his first service, at the age of 16, at Tresillian (see Truro).

TRESMEER
Charles Wesley preached in the parish church several times between 1744 and 1746, and John Wesley seven times during the years 1745-51. On the last occasion (with his wife in the congregation) he read prayers and preached. The church was rebuilt c.1880. The Bible Christians held an all-day open-air meeting on Tresmeer Down during their 1820 Conference at Launceston.

TRETHOSA
Jack Clemo, the poet of the clay country, celebrated the centenary of this Bible Christian chapel in 1976 with the evocative lines:

Roots of my story quiver
In this corner-guarding Bethel
I think how my bubbly,
    field-toughened grandfather
Clapped and shouted behind
    the pulpit,
And how a grave-toned minister
Marked the ablation on my face
As my infant eyes blinked at the
    communion rail.
And there, fifty odd years later,
I spoke vows at the end of a
    twisted lane
Where I entered, bride-blessed,
    a straight, spurred union.

A room in the chapel is set aside to commemorate Clemo's life.

TREVEAN SW550290, Perranuthnoe.
John Wesley is said to have preached here. Harry Carter, the converted smuggler, became a member here (see Fowey and Rinsey). The former Wesleyan chapel closed in 1938, and was latterly an agricultural store, but seems now to be disused.

TREVEIGHAN, Michaelstow
A Bible Christian proprietary chapel with its owner's initials on the date

stone – 'E.H. 1828'. Edward Hocken was a lay advisor to the Bible Christians on educational matters. In the schoolroom is a framed circuit plan of 1863-64 on which the list of preachers is headed by the name of Samuel Pollard, the father of the China missionary of the same name (see Camelford).

TREWALDER SX074822

The chapel closed in 2000. A desk formerly in the schoolroom is now among the CMHA collection at Carharrack (q.v.). It is said to have been used by Wesley, possibly when writing class tickets, a few of which have survived.

TREWELLARD

Within the chapel, which closed in 2003, there was a memorial to the men who lost their lives in the Levant Mine disaster in 1919. There is a possibility that the memorial might find its way down to the Levant Mine National Trust site, which is further down the lane beside the chapel. There the Man Engine Shaft in which the disaster occurred can be viewed. The archway at the Green Court on which Wesley is said to have struck his hand forcibly to express his disapproval of the Calvinists has unfortunately been demolished.

TREWINT SX220804

The Wesley Cottage, or Isbell Cottage, stands a few yards north of the A30 about eight miles west of Launceston on the west side of a very minor small loop road off the old A30 through the village; at the north end of the road a small museum sign points down to the cottage. From Launceston leave the dual carriageway at the point marked 'Five Lanes' and/or 'Altarnun' and, beyond the underpass, turn left into Trewint. From Bodmin leave the A30 by the slip road to Five Lanes and Altarnun.

The A30 through Cornwall follows the line of the eighteenth-century coach road across the moor which was a mere track when John Wesley and his three companions first entered the county in 1743. Wesley was riding with William Shepherd, but John Nelson and John Downes, who were travelling 'ride and tie' with one horse between them, stopped at Trewint and asked for refreshment at 'the house with the stone porch'. They were made welcome by Elizabeth Isbell, the stonemason's wife, and Nelson returned to the cottage when he was leaving Cornwall some weeks later. He was entertained by Digory and Elizabeth Isbell and addressed some 300 people at 7 a.m. the following morning.

John Wesley stayed at the house a number of times and his host, after reading about the visit of the prophet Elisha to the Shunammite woman (2 Kings 4:8-11) added two rooms to the cottage ('the Prophets' Chamber') for the use of Wesley and his preachers. Services were held at the stone porch and a small society was formed which met regularly at the cottage. Early in the twentieth century the cottage fell into a ruinous state and by 1948 was in danger of being demolished. Memories of John Wesley still lingered there, however, and largely through the insight and organising ability of Stanley Sowton (see Rilla Mill) the cottage was purchased for £50, expertly restored by Sir George Oakley of Bristol at a cost of £1,000, placed on a trust and, on Wesley Day 1950, opened to the public. A continuous stream of visitors have since found their way to Trewint. On the Sunday afternoon nearest to Wesley Day (24 May) a service is held in the porch, followed by an evening service in Launceston.

The house at Trewint consists of the original cottage, part of which is privately occupied, but the two rooms added by Digory Isbell are open daily from dawn to dusk to welcome all comers. The passage leads to the downstairs room with its open fireplace at which John Wesley must have warmed his hands and sat down to write his letters which he did almost daily. The upper room, once the bedroom, contains items of Wesleyana including a copy of Burkitt's *Notes on the New Testament* which John Nelson

used as his pillow when he was at St Ives in 1743.

In the Pilgrims' Garden (opened 1958), opposite the front porch, is a replica of the sundial at Birstall, Yorkshire, made by John Nelson, and a garden seat presented by Mr H. Guy Chester of Muswell Hill. Incongruous in that position is a modern stone Communion table from the closed chapel at Minions.

TREWOON SW995527
Both the Wesleys preached at St Mewan, probably on the Green at Trewoon by the railway arch on the road from St Austell to Newquay. A large stone nearby used to be pointed out as the place where, it was said, 'Wesley and Whitefield stood and preached the Gospel of the grace of God'.

TRURO
Wesley avoided preaching in Truro until 1760, choosing to leave the town to the ministrations of Samuel Walker, the curate of St Mary's, an evangelical and a Calvinist. In later years he preached in Boscawen Street at the spot now marked by a wall plaque facing the war memorial, and also by the West Bridge (now Victoria Square). The first Methodist society room was down the 'ope' in Boscawen Street, opposite the entrance to King Street; the first preaching house, in which Wesley himself preached, was on the site of what is now Walsingham Place. A more substantial chapel was built in Kenwyn Street in 1795 (see The Salvation Army Citadel below).

The cathedral has a number of Methodist associations: (1) The Wesley Window near the west end of the south nave aisle shows John Wesley in a purple gown with Charles Wesley and Samuel Walker, the curate of Truro, somewhat incongruously, sitting at his feet, and below this, Wesley preaching in Gwennap Pit. The window is a memorial to Captain James Dunn, a friend of John Wesley (see Mevagissey) and his two sons, one of whom was the Methodist reformer, Samuel Dunn (see Camborne). (2) A memorial in the south aisle, to Bishop Joseph Wellington Hunkin (1887-1950), who had previously been a local preacher in the Truro Circuit (see Tresillian). (3) The Baptistry is a memorial to the missionary, Henry Martyn, for whom the Truro Methodists always had a high regard. (4) In the north transept is a memorial to John Couch Adams, the discoverer of Neptune (see Laneast and Tregeare). The Cornwall Council of Churches, in which Methodism takes an active part, was formed at a service in the cathedral in 1970.

Wesley paid a morning visit to Kenwyn Vicarage, now the Epiphany House, in 1787, and thought it was 'a house fit for a nobleman'. The vicar, Richard Milles, was a grandson of Archbishop Potter who had ordained John Wesley some 60 years before. The house later became the bishop's residence, and in 1909 Bishop Stubbs had a replica of Burnard's head of Wesley (see Altarnun) made in Truro and placed in the chapel. Also in the house is a statue of the Virgin and Child made by a Roman Catholic sculptor and presented as an ecumenical gesture by the Revd C. Kingsley Williams, a retired Methodist missionary.

Truro Methodist Church (1830), formerly St Mary Clement and before that St Mary's, has an imposing Grecian style front. Among its memorials is one to its first minister, William Hayman, a native of Stratton. One of the windows in the gallery is a memorial – unexpectedly – to General Gordon of Khartoum. In the vestry are two framed cards bearing the signatures of the Presidents of the Wesleyan, and later the Methodist, Conference who have preached at St Mary's from 1887-1989. The chapel was extensively modernized in 2000.

The former UMFC church in St George's Road has a Gothic façade denuded of its pinnacles. It was opened in 1881 and closed in 1996 becoming a Roman Catholic school. The society joined with St Mary Clement to form Truro Methodist Church.

The former Bible Christian church in St Clement Street, dating from 1835, is now the offices of a firm of wine importers, a curious change of use for one of the most staunch teetotal branches of Methodism. The Bible Christian Conference met here in 1842 and 1879. The chapel closed in 1974, joining with St Mary's to form St Mary Clement Church.

The Methodist New Connexion arrived in the town in 1834, after a dispute within the ranks of the Wesleyans. Numbers withdrew, and invited the

New Connexion to adopt them. Ebenezer Chapel was built on Castle Street, but on union in 1907 no minister was appointed, and the circuit was rapidly absorbed by the Bible Christians. No trace of the chapel remains.

Primitive Methodism struggled to establish itself in Truro, but after several attempts a former Mormon fellowship became the core of a fairly stable society in 1862. In 1878 they built the Early English Gothic chapel in Kenwyn Street, which persisted through high and low periods until 1941. After being closed for some while the building became the home of the ex-Wesleyan City Mission, until it closed in 1976. The building is now a Meadery – the second of the formerly staunchly teetotal branch chapels in the city to succumb to 'the evil drink'!

The Salvation Army Citadel in Kenwyn Street occupies part of the old Wesleyan chapel (1795-1831), later used by the Free Methodists from 1876-1881.

In the Courtney Library at the Royal Cornwall Museum in River Street is the extensive Shaw Collection of books, files and manuscripts relating to Cornish Methodism and the Bible Christians, including three Wesley letters and the manuscript journal of Mary O'Bryan (later Mary Thorne). An oil painting of Billy Bray by Stanley S. Bennett is in the Art Gallery collection. The museum also possesses a watch and teapot which belonged to Captain Harry Carter (see Rinsey). Bishop Phillpott's Library at Diocesan House, Kenwyn, has an important collection of books about Wesley and Early Methodism. The County Record Office, Old County Hall, which is the repository for official Methodist records, also has many other items of Methodist ephemera.

Truro School (1880) was opened at No. 4 Strangways Terrace with 25 boarders and ten day boys, and moved to its present commanding site overlooking the city in 1882. Today it has over 882 pupils, of whom 93 are borders and 312 are girls. Mr A. Lowry Creed, MA, the headmaster from 1946-59, was Vice-President of the Methodist Conference 1962-63, and Mr Derek W. Burrell, MA, the headmaster from 1959-86, was Vice-President 1987-88. Its preparatory school, Treliske, was previously the home of Sir George Smith, an eminent Methodist and educationalist.

The Chairman of the Cornwall Methodist District has lived in Truro since Methodist Union in 1932. The present Chairman is the Revd Dr Canon Chris Blake. As an expression of the growing ecumenical spirit between the District and the Diocese, his predecessor the Revd Stephen Dawes had been made a Canon of the Cathedral, and the honour has been extended to the new Chairman.

ST TUDY

Charles Wesley preached at St Tudy, either inside or outside the church, in 1746, supported by the vicars of St Gennys and Tresmeer. The scene can have changed little over the years. On the left of the path from the south-east gate of the churchyard to the church porch there is a headstone memorial to William Oke, a Wesleyan missionary to the West Indies, who lost his life in the wreck of the *Maria* mail-boat off the coast of Antigua in 1826.

TWELVEHEADS

A neat and well-kept Wesleyan chapel, built in 1828. Its predecessor was a smaller one which Billy Bray attended as a child, along with his grandfather, who was 'one of the first Methodees' there (see Billy Bray Country).

VOGUEBELOTH SW677434

The former Wesleyan chapel (1866) closed in 2003, but one of its features was a leaders' pew with reading desk attached standing at the front of the centre block of pews, a not uncommon feature in Cornish chapels. The Sunday school opposite on the north side of the road has been occupied by the Seventh Day Adventists for several years.

WADEBRIDGE

Egloshayle Church was the scene of the ministry of the Revd Sir Harry Trelawny of Trelawne, near Looe. Originally an Anglican, Sir Harry became a Congregational minister and built a church at Looe before returning to the Church of England and becoming vicar of Egloshayle. At that time he received a letter from John Wesley congratulating him that his prejudices against the Church of England had been removed. While at Egloshayle, from 1793-1804, he gave guidance in spiritual things to a group of young men with whom he had twice-weekly meetings for prayer and study in which he made use of Wesley's sermons and hymns. This group included Malachi Davey (1756-1828) and Alexander Menhinick (1775-1812) who were to become leaders in the Camelford Circuit and in Wadebridge Methodism. The table tomb of the latter, in the north-west corner of the churchyard, has an interesting epitaph which was composed by the vicar, Sir Harry's successor. The gravestone of Malachi Davey stands close by. Sir Harry's spiritual pilgrimage did not end when he left Egloshayle, for he later became a Roman Catholic priest and died in Italy.

In the Methodist church (formerly Trinity) is a memorial tablet to Ann West (1783-1872), a Wesleyan class leader whose life story is told in *Living Christianity*, by Mary Higgs. She lived through the turmoil of the disruption of the circuit in 1834-35 (see Boscastle) and took part in rebuilding the Wesleyan society at Wadebridge. The tablet reminds the cóngregation of 'her consistent piety and unselfish benevolence [which] secured for her the Christian esteem and regard of all who knew her. She was a wise counsellor and a sympathetic friend and [was] connected by membership with the Wesleyan Church of this place for 70 years … Soli Deo Gloria'.

The recent history of the chapels in Wadebridge is complex. The ex-Bible Christian chapel in Trevanion Road closed in 1951, only to reopen in 1958. In 1961 Trinity, the ex-Wesleyan chapel, closed when the society merged with the ex-UMFC society at Egloshayle

Road. Yet when this chapel was demolished in 1969 due to road widening, the society reverted to Trinity. In 1970 the ex-Bible Christian society joined the Trinity society and Trevanion Road closed dfor worship but continued to be used most days of the week.

WALL, Gwinear

According to an old and reliable tradition John Wesley stayed and slept at the home of the wheelwright, Francis Hale, and his wife Ann. Only a fragment remains of the wall of their house, some 15 yards along the road to the west of the chapel.

WARBSTOW BURROW SX202908

This Iron Age fort, now in the care of the local council, was the scene of many Methodist open-air gatherings in the early part of the nineteenth century. It was claimed by a writer as early as 1838 that Wesley and Whitefield had both preached there, though there is no confirmation of this in their journals. William O'Bryan spoke there from a farm cart at the annual Wesleyan missionary meeting which was held on Whit Tuesday each year, supported by the three contiguous circuits, Launceston, Camelford and Holsworthy.

WEEK ST MARY

Wesley preached in the parish church, at the invitation of the Revd John Turner, on at least six occasions. The pulpit he used is still there. He also preached at Mill House near Week Orchard of which he wrote in 1757:'The house stands in the midst of orchards and meadows surrounded by gently rising hills', and in 1765: 'We had a pleasant ride to Mill House.' Week Orchard where, it is claimed, Wesley was entertained, is in the midst of orchards, and there was a preaching house at Mill House, half a mile distant, until it was replaced by Titson Chapel in 1882.

By 1815 Week Orchard was the home of the Wesleyan circuit steward, Richard Spettigue, who threw in his lot with William O'Bryan and helped him in the formation of the Bible Christians. It was when he was sure of Spettigue's support that O'Bryan wrote:'On October 1st 1815 I entered on my circuit at Mary-Week and Hex.' In so doing he brought the new denomination into being. The first Bible Christian Communion Service and its first local preachers' meeting were held at Week Orchard.

WENDRON

John Wesley preached several times at Porkellis and also at Tolcarne, where on one occasion he was pushed off a wall. An annual service was formerly held at Tolcarne Rock to mark the place of his preaching in 1745. Wesley attended a service in Wendron Church that year. Canon G.H. Doble, the Celtic scholar, was the vicar here from 1925-45. In one of his books he drew a parallel between the ministries of John Wesley and the seventeenth-century Breton missioner, Fr Julien Maunoir.

WHITEMOOR

This former Bible Christian chapel (1875) in the St Austell china clay country has, at the back of the building, Cornwall's smallest preaching pit. It is documented from 1871 and so predates the chapel.

The pit consists of circles, or rather segments of circles, of grassy seats and, as at Indian Queens, it was used mainly for Sunday school events.

WHITSTONE
The first Bible Christian chapel was opened at Boot, where it still stands, in 1835. James Thorne preached on the foundation stone of the present church in 1863 and it was opened in the following year by Frederick W. Bourne. Thorne was the leader of the Bible Christians through most of their 92-year history, and Bourne for the last 30 years of the denomination.

ZENNOR
Both the Wesleys attended services at Zennor Church a number of times between 1746 and 1760, and John preached 'under the churchyard wall' – the obvious place would have been the steps. John Nelson, who accompanied Wesley on his first Cornish tour, preached standing on, or by, the massive Trewey rock, above the Wayside Museum. On the inside wall of the church tower are the memorials to Wesley's hosts, the Thomases of Treen.

The Wesleyan chapel closed in 1973 and is now a summer cafeteria and backpackers' hostel for the Coastal Path.

The Trewey Rock

Billy Bray Country

Billy Bray (1794-1868) was a tin miner, at first a hard-drinking and swearing man, whose oaths, they said, came straight from hell, but who after his conversion in 1823 became a well-known and much-loved local preacher among the Bible Christians. Remembered for his quaint humour and sanctified witticisms he became, after his death, a Cornish folk-hero. Dressed in his ill-fitting black coat and neckerchief he was often seen dancing along the lanes because he was too happy to walk. 'If they were to put me into a barrel, I would shout glo-a-ry out through the bung-hole!' he said. F.W. Bourne's biography of Billy Bray, *The King's Son*, first published in 1871, has passed through innumerable editions and kept his memory alive to the present day. A new 'life' based on his manuscript Journals was published in the autumn of 2004.

Only a small portion of the cottage in which he lived and died, and that in a sorry state, can still be seen. It is on the north side of the lane from Twelveheads to Cross Lanes (SW762424), adjoined on the downhill side by stables. A painting of the house by his nephew, John Verran, is in the CMHA Museum at Carharrack. A few yards up the hill beyond the house is a lane leading south east to Bethel. The original Bethel Chapel is now reduced to a hardly noticeable piece of walling at the bottom of the hedge, just inside the gateway which leads to the later Bethel Chapel, although it is almost impossible to identify. This chapel, built in 1842 and closed in 1962, is now an artist's studio. Billy Bray was the builder of the first Bethel and had some part in the building of the second.

KERLEY DOWNS CHAPEL (SW765437)

Billy Bray also built this chapel, which has become his chief memorial, and was one of its first trustees. Popularly known as Three Eyes because it originally had three windows, the chapel was built in 1836. The chapel possesses an oil painting by Stanley S. Bennett (1964) of Billy Bray based on a photograph of c.1860. A framed copy of the portrait is hung behind the pulpit and may be compared with the slightly different one by the same artist in the County Art Gallery in Truro. In the chapel is a chair with the words 'Billy Bray 1839' cut into the seat. The chapel was closed in 1982 and the lease surrendered to Lord Falmouth who then granted it to a new 'Billy Bray Memorial Trust'. The chapel was rededicated by the Chairman of the District and reopened by Lady Falmouth in 1984. It is usually open during daylight hours, May to mid-October, approximately 10 a.m. to 5.30 p.m.

BALDHU CHURCH

The church nearby, now closed and boarded up, was the scene of Parson Haslam's conversion in his own pulpit, an event which brought much joy to Billy Bray who went round to the vicarage and danced Haslam and his servants around the house for very joy. Billy Bray's grave is in the increasingly overgrown churchyard immediately beside the church on its south side, and is marked by an obelisk which was erected in 1880. The inscription reads:

In memory of William,
better known as Billy Bray,
who died at Twelveheads,
May 25, 1868,
aged seventy-three years.

By his sanctified wit, Christian simplicity, fervid faith and many self-denying labours he commended himself to a wide circle of friends while living, and the published records since his death of his memorable sayings and doings has made his name familiar as a household word in our own and other lands. He was a Local Preacher with the Bible Christians forty-three years.

whitewash on the north side of Consols Road just before the junction with United Road. It can also be seen, across the valley, from Crofthandy. Billy Bray's privileged position among his fellow trustees was written into the chapel deed – he was to have two votes at their meetings. Great Deliverance was superseded by a chapel in the village in 1874 and, in 1885, by the Billy Bray Memorial Church (built partly from the proceeds of a lottery). It was demolished in 1987. A few exhibits relating to Billy Bray, including his chair and china dogs, can be seen at the Museum of Cornish Methodism in the village. (See also Carharrack, Hicks Mill and Twelveheads.)

Billy Bray Obelisk at Baldhu

GREET DELIVERANCE CHAPEL
Carharrack (SW739418)

The lower part of the chapel, built by Billy Bray in 1840, is now a farm building still showing signs of

William O'Bryan Country

GUNWEN FARM
Luxulyan (SX051607)
The birthplace of William Bryant (later O'Bryan) the founder of the Bible Christians. He was born, as he said, 'under the shadow of Helman Tor'. The farmhouse today is a Victorian rebuild of the older home of the Bryants, but much of the granite walling of the older house can still be seen in the outbuildings. The marker was placed on the wall on the 200th anniversary of O'Bryan's birth and was unveiled by Miss Patricia Slade of Chawleigh, one of his descendants. It reads:

William O'Bryan
1778-1868
the founder of the Bible Christians
was born here on
February 6th 1778

O'Bryan's daughter, Mary, the Bible Christian 'Maiden Preacher', was born at Gunwen on 3 April 1807.

The farmhouse is private property.

LUXULYAN CHURCH
O'Bryan was baptized here on 24 April 1778. The family occupied the Tredinnick pew. Like his father, O'Bryan held various parish offices; he was one of 'the twelve men' (the select vestry) of the parish and was in turn Overseer of the Poor and churchwarden. There are four slate headstones to various members of the Bryant family close to the south-east corner of the church in the graveyard, which show the variations of the family name. Burials within the church were still remembered in the 1780s and William Bryant senior would point out the family places of burial as he sat in his pew.

GUNWEN CHAPEL
The plaque over the door was placed there in 1978 and unveiled by Mrs D.M. Moody of Tavistock, a great-great-granddaughter of William O'Bryan. It is inscribed:

In Piam Memoriam
William O'Bryan
Born at Gunwen Farm,
February 6th 1778
Gave the land and helped
to build the
first chapel on this site, c. 1796
founded the Bible Christian Church
at
Week St. Mary,
1st October 1815
Died at New York,
January 8th 1868

It was in this chapel, which William O'Bryan had helped to build, that he was expelled from the Wesleyan society in 1810. The chapel, of course, continued in the Wesleyan tradition until Methodist Union in 1932. In the burial ground is the slate carved gravestone of O'Bryan's child, Ebenezer William, who died of spotted fever in 1808.

INNIS (SX026622)
O'Bryan's Quaker forefathers – the Groses – farmed Innis, and a Quaker

burial ground was already there when O'Bryan bought the land and built the small chapel in 1820. On the Communion table is a glass case which contains O'Bryan's Bible, and a few of his sermon notes. There is also a class ticket issued to his daughter, Mary, and a copy of the 1851 edition of the Bible Christian hymn book, open at his mother's funeral hymn. Thomasine Bryant died at Launceston and was buried at Innis in 1821. O'Bryan erected the gravestone in 1836 (see Fraddon). It is the third stone from the door, near the chapel. Other gravestones of interest include those of Henry Reed (Bible Christian President, 1844) and 'Uncle Will' Alllin (1760-1845) of Little Torrington, Devon, an 'itinerant prayer and class leader'. The chapel and its surroundings convey a feeling of remoteness which was real enough when members of the congregation carried lanterns across the moor to light their way to chapel.

Today it is close to the Innis roundabout at the western end of the Bodmin bypass. To reach the chapel turn left off the A30 immediately after leaving the roundabout. A T-junction is immediately encountered. The chapel key can be obtained by turning left and following the road about 400 yards to Castle Hill, the first farm on the right. The chapel is found by retracing the route, over the T-junction, past the houses, and on down the track. The top part of the track, through the gate labelled Innis Chapel was named Lynne's Walk after it was renovated in 1993 in memory of Miss Lynne Francis.

The development of O'Bryan's work and the formation of the Bible Christians can be traced from Week St Mary and Launcells in North Cornwall and across the Devon border to Shebbear (see p. 72). For later Bible Christian expansion see Boscastle, Padstow, Camelford and 'Across the Tamar'.

Across the Tamar

SHEBBEAR, Devon

In the burial ground of Lake Chapel are the gravestones of Samuel Thorne, Printer, and his wife, the former Mary O'Bryan (1807-83) (see St Austell and William O'Bryan Country).

BRISTOL

The New Room (1739) was the centre of early Methodism in Bristol. From here the Wesleys and many of their helpers set out for Cornwall. Joseph Turner, a sea captain, who was a member of the Bristol society, visited St Ives in 1743 and discovered a 'religious society' meeting there. It may have been this discovery that decided John Wesley to extend his work into Cornwall (see St Ives). On the inner window of the Common Room is scratched with a diamond a piece of pious graffiti which reads:

On brittle glass I grave my name
A follower of the bleeding Lamb
But thou can'st shew a nobler art
And grave thy name upon my heart.
Francis Woolf

Woolf had been engaged by Wesley as one of his travelling preachers when he was at Redruth. After travelling for a few years Woolf returned there and set up in business in the town (see Redruth). In a case in the Adam Clarke room is the crown-piece which Wesley gave to young William Chenhalls at St Just. The New Room archives also contain other items relating to Cornish Methodism, notably a Gwithian Chapel deed, 1771, class tickets issued at

Mousehole c.1760, and various letters.

The New Room Library holds the collection of the Bulletins of the regional Branch Societies of the Wesley Historical Society. An index is available.

In the City Museum and Art Gallery are two pieces of English Delftware which once belonged to two of Wesley's hosts in Cornwall. The first is a plate with a print of a lamb and the inscription 'Jos Hosken Esq, Carines 1771' (see Cubert). The other is a dish inscribed 'Richard Wood, Port Isaac, 1764' (see Port Isaac).

LONDON

John Murlin (1722-99), the early preacher from St Stephen in Brannel, is buried in Wesley's tomb at Wesley's Chapel, City Road. Also in the chapel yard is the grave of Peter Jaco (1729-81) the former Newlyn fisherman. The stone bearing his epitaph, written by Charles Wesley, has been recut; it reads:

Fisher of men, ordain'd by Christ alone,
Immortal souls he for his Saviour
won;
With loving faith, and calmly-potent zeal,
Perform'd and suffer'd the
Redeemer's will
Steadfast in all the storms of life remain'd
And in the good old ship the
haven gain'd.

Among those named on the large headstone of The Preachers' Grave is Richard Treffry (1771-1842) of Tregony, the President of the Conference in 1833. The early Bible Christians had a preaching place in Tabernacle Walk behind Wesley's Chapel as early as 1823. A poster announcing that James Thorne and 'A Female' would be preaching at Ebenezer Chapel, Old Street, can be seen in the Museum of Methodism in the crypt.

MANCHESTER
In the Methodist Archives and Research Centre, The John Rylands University Library of Manchester, Deansgate, Manchester are many Cornish Methodist items including the MS Journals of William O'Bryan and Billy Bray and the Lewis H. Court Bible Christian Collection. A descriptive catalogue of the Court Collection was issued by the Library in 1995.

NEW YORK
William and Catherine O'Bryan died in New York and are buried in the Greenwood Cemetery, Brooklyn. Their two gravestones, marked on the back 'Father' and 'Mother', show the family reversion to the name Bryant.

CANADA
Mount Rundle in Alberta and the Rundle Memorial Church (United Church of Canada) at Banff are memorials to Robert Terril Rundle (see Mylor).

CHINA
The farthest outreach of Cornish Methodism is to be found in the Yunnan province of China, where the Miao tribesmen erected a massive stone memorial to Samuel Pollard (see Camelford) on the river bank.